OCTOBER/NOVEMBER 1978   Volume 29/Number 6

AMERICAN HERITAGE

Editor, Alvin M. Josephy, Jr.

Managing Editor, Geoffrey C. Ward

Design Director, Massimo Vignelli
Art Director, Elizabeth-Anne Wilbur

Board of Editors, E. M. Halliday, *Chairman,*
Bruce Catton, Barbara Klaw, Elizabeth
Oettinger, Brenda Savard, T. H. Watkins

Picture Editors, Carla Davidson, *Chief;*
Jane Colihan, Villette Harris

Copy Editor, Carol Smillie

Editorial Assistants, Margaret Keeley,
Mary Elizabeth Wise

Production Manager, Carlos A. Aguilar

Contributing Editors, Allan L. Damon,
Oliver Jensen, Joan Paterson Kerr,
Richard F. Snow, Bernard A. Weisberger

Advisory Board, Henry Steele Commager,
Marshall B. Davidson, John A. Garraty,
Eugene D. Genovese, William H.
Goetzmann, Archibald Hanna, Arthur M.
Schlesinger, Jr., Thomas Vaughan

London Office, Rosemary L. Klein

Sponsored by American Association
for State and Local History • Society
of American Historians

AMERICAN HERITAGE
PUBLISHING COMPANY

Chairman of the Board, Samuel P. Reed
President and Publisher, Rhett Austell
Editor in Chief—Magazines, Alvin M. Josephy, Jr.
Administrative Editor—Magazines, Brenda Savard
Consulting Editor, J. H. Plumb
Editorial Art Director, Murray Belsky
Treasurer, Frederick A. Gunzel
Catalogue Sales Director, Ernest S. Quick
Promotion Art Director, David A. Van Inwegen
Circulation Director, Donald B. Barrows, Jr.
Production Director, Elbert Burr

AMERICAN HERITAGE, The Magazine of History,
is published every two months by American Heritage
Publishing Co., Inc.; editorial and executive offices,
10 Rockefeller Plaza, N.Y., N.Y. 10020. Secretary,
Frederick A. Gunzel. Correspondence about
subscriptions should go to American Heritage
Subscription Office, 383 West Center St., Marion,
Ohio 43302. Single copies: $6. Annual subscriptions:
$21 in U.S.; $23 in Canada; $26 elsewhere. A 10-year
Index of Vols. VI-XV is available at $7.50; 5-year Index
of Vols. XVI-XX at $7.50; 5-year Index of Vols. XXI-
XXV at $7.50; 1-year Index of Vol. XXVI at $5;
1-year Index of Vol. XXVII at $5; 1-year Index of
Vol. XXVIII at $5.

AMERICAN HERITAGE considers but assumes no
responsibility for unsolicited materials; these require
return postage. Title registered U.S. Patent Office.
Second-class postage paid at New York, N.Y., and at
additional mailing offices.

Postmaster: Please send Form 3579 to AMERICAN
HERITAGE, 381 West Center Street, Marion, Ohio
43302.

AMERICAN HERITAGE has been selected by the
Library of Congress for reproduction on recordings
called Talking Books, distributed free by regional
libraries in the U.S. to those unable to use
conventional print because of a visual or physical
handicap. For information write the Library of
Congress, Division for the Blind and Physically
Handicapped, 1291 Taylor St., N.W., Washington,
D.C. 20542.

Just as this issue of AMERICAN HERITAGE *went to press we had bad news from Michigan: our distinguished senior editor Bruce Catton, who was intimately associated with the magazine from its beginning, died there near his boyhood home on August 28. Worldwide fame as a Civil War historian never affected the unassuming friendliness Bruce exercised toward his editorial colleagues, or his down-to-earth judgments on manuscripts, or the consummate ease with which he edited articles for publication. He will be missed enormously in this office. We are planning a fuller tribute to him in a forthcoming issue; meanwhile we want to quote, in memoriam, a paragraph from an essay Bruce Catton wrote for the first issue of* AMERICAN HERITAGE *in 1954, and which we still think of as the quintessence of our editorial credo.*

The fabric of American life is a seamless web. Everything fits in somewhere. History is a continuous process; it extends far back into the past, and it will go on—in spite of today's uneasy qualms—far into the future. As editors of this magazine we can think of no more eternally fascinating task than that of examining this continuous process on a day-to-day basis. Sometimes we shall talk about great men and what they did, and sometimes we shall talk about the doings of wholly obscure people who made the great men possible. But always we intend to deal with that great, unfinished, and illogically inspiring story of the American people doing and being and becoming. Our American heritage is greater than any one of us. It can express itself in very homely truths; in the end, it can lift up our eyes beyond the glow in the sunset skies.

COVER
Although Americans were keen hunters and fishermen from colonial times (this Currier & Ives lithograph dates from 1852), it was only after the Civil War that a combination of affluence, leisure, and male chauvinism gave rise to the species Sportsman in large numbers. In an article starting on page 94, John Mitchell examines the haunts and habits of this tweedy breed in the days of its most de luxe and elaborate predatory excursions.

THE HARRY T. PETERS COLLECTION, MUSEUM OF THE CITY OF NEW YORK

CONTENTS

INHALE!...

Summer flight: the cover of Bernarr Macfadden's strenuous Physical Culture *magazine featured this handsome, energetic pair in August, 1914.*

INTERNATIONAL SPORTS AND GAMES RESEARCH COLLECTION, NOTRE DAME

EXHALE!...INHALE!...EXHALE!...

Most people paid scant attention to deliberate strenuous exercise before the 1880's. Since then the pendulum has swung from pro to con and back again.

by Paul Lancaster

All you joggers out there dodging garbage trucks at dawn, listen to this: "I am fully convinced that exercise is bosh.... Find ways to exert yourself and you find ways to harm yourself.... Do not stand when you can sit; or sit when you can lie down; or just lie down when you can nap. Do not run if you can walk.... To have a strong heart it is essential to give up all unnecessary exercise."

In a day when sixty-year-olds train for marathons, middle-aged cyclists rack up the miles on their ten-speeds, and tennis players of all shapes and sizes crowd the courts, the advice sounds strange. But it was written little more than a generation ago by Dr. Peter Steincrohn, a reputable physician. His view was shared widely at the time. For anyone beyond the flush of youth, strenuous exercise was thought to carry the risk of heart strain. Now most physicians hold the precise opposite to be true: *failure* to engage regularly in vigorous exercise is believed to increase the risk of heart disease.

This about-face is only one of the periodic changes in direction that have occurred since Americans in large numbers began to concern themselves with exercise for the sake of health. That doesn't seem to have happened until sometime toward the end of the nineteenth century. There had always been a few, of course, who kept playing games—cricket, rounders, and, later, baseball—after school days were over. The well-to-do took up golf and tennis in the last decades of the century. Young Theodore Roosevelt, an awkward but enthusiastic tennis player, battled through ninety-one games one day in 1882.

Cycling had its devotees beginning with the introduction of the high-wheeler in the 1870's, and there were also some early advocates of rigorous physical training routines. German immigrants of the mid-1800's transplanted the Turners, athletic societies devoted to gymnastics on rings, bars, and vaulting horses. In the 1870's some colleges started formal physical education classes where students tossed medicine balls and performed drills designed to improve posture. Even in the years just before his death at the age of eighty-three in 1878, William Cullen Bryant rose early to heft dumbbells for an hour and then strode the three miles from his house in lower Manhattan to the *New York Evening Post*. There, scorning the newfangled elevator, he ran up ten flights of stairs to his office, where he sometimes stopped at the door to seize the lintel and raise and lower himself by his arms several times.

But for most people of that era the physical demands of ordinary life were quite enough, and the notion that they should seek out extra work for their muscles would have seemed bizarre. That was particularly true for the great majority of Americans who still lived in rural areas—almost 75 per cent in 1870—and for whom heavy farm labor from dawn to dusk was often the rule. But it also held true for many city dwellers. They drew water, chopped wood, walked to work and church. Understandably, technological advances that saved human effort—elevators, streetcars, telephones, running water—were seen as undiluted blessings.

Attitudes toward exercise were changing as 1890 approached, however. Urbanization was steadily reducing the proportion of Americans who had to spend their days wrestling plows and pitching hay. "Americans went indoors to serve machines, stand behind counters, or sit at desks," observes one historian. When a handful of self-proclaimed "experts" on physical fitness began spreading the message that the "nineteenth-century method of living" was making the nation soft, they found a receptive audience, and their numbers proliferated. "Professors" of physical culture opened gymnasiums where businessmen paid to swing Indian clubs and "in-hale!...ex-hale!" to the cadence of instructors. Doctors, who were often scornful of the physical culturists muscling into what they considered their purview, offered their own regimens. Books and magazine articles poured forth promoting one new system of exercise after another and exhorting readers to shape up in tones so stirring that it is almost impossible to dip into their musty pages today without instinctively squaring the shoulders and taking a deep breath.

If a man feels he is getting soft, the most obvious solution is to acquire a handsome pair of biceps, and the early exercise manuals stressed straightforward muscle building. One was entitled *How to Get Strong*. Another demanded: "Why be weakly?" The goal was more modest than the exaggerated musculature of today's body-building cultists; one set of arm exercises was designed to produce arms "which look well either in rowing or exercising costume, that is, with nothing on them, or which set off a well-cut coat to great advantage." But the authors themselves were nevertheless pretty impressive specimens who were not at all reticent about their own physical accomplishments—one, for example, invited two-hundred-pounders to don heavy boots and take a running jump onto his abdomen—and the clear implication was that readers could achieve similar physiques if only they would pay attention.

The recommended exercise was demanding, often calling for the use of weights and other strengthening equipment. In the nineties many bedrooms were graced by A. G. Spalding & Bros. Victor No. 5 Machine, a contraption of pulleys and weights that attached to the wall. In the same decade, J. R. Judd, a professor of physical culture with a luxuriant handlebar mustache, published *Always Strong and Happy*, a course that required a whole array of equipment manufactured by Judd, including dumbbells weighing up to forty pounds, a racklike affair called the Extensor, and his Columbia Parlor General Exercising and Rowing Machine. After punishing himself with this paraphernalia, the victim was instructed to plunge into a cold bath, which was the standard conclusion for most of the exercise programs.

The best known of the early body builders was Bernarr Macfadden. In 1898, when he was a sleek-muscled, narcissistic thirty-year-old, Macfadden published a five-cent pamphlet called *Physical Culture*. It evolved into a monthly magazine with a circulation of half a million and helped make Macfadden a cult figure among health faddists. Macfadden, who in time built a publishing enterprise that also included such magazines as *True Story* and *True Romance* and a sleazy newspaper known formally as the *New York Evening Graphic* but informally as the *Pornographic*, presented a body-building scheme, using a contrivance of pulleys and cords, in a book in 1900. Sprinkled among nude or near-nude photographs of Macfadden posing on a pedestal or on a leopard skin were stern admonitions: "Clear your system of accumulated corruption from inactivity, and live! . . . If you are weak,

there is absolutely no excuse for your continuing so."

Macfadden's methods worked for him. He lived to the age of eighty-seven, and he celebrated his seventy-fifth birthday by standing on his head during an interview and his eighty-third by making a parachute jump into the Hudson River. But in the eyes of many, muscle building had a couple of serious disadvantages. One was that it entailed considerable effort. The other was that no matter how hard they heaved and strained, when most men stood before a mirror—Macfadden recommended exercising there—they were never going to see a Greek god.

So another crop of experts came to the rescue with the good news that large muscles were out of date. They were contemptuous of the muscle builders. "The ordinary gymnasium 'professor' knows no more about the principles of bodily development than he does about ancient Coptic," scoffed a physician named Latson in 1910. Another doctor, writing in *Harper's*, warned that muscle building was positively dangerous to the health. Backing came from a 1910 editorial in the *New York Times* deploring the emphasis on "brute strength" in physical education. "The cultivation of huge muscles belonged to the hunting, grazing, peasant, and warrior stages of civilization," said the *Times*.

To replace arduous muscle building, the doctors and others proposed less taxing calisthenics. There were variations in the systems; one school held, for example, that touching the toes without bending the knees was beneficial, while a rival camp insisted that if God had intended man to do that, He would not have provided knee joints. But for the most part the movements were similar—stretch, twist, turn, bend. They were the sort of mild exercises a lot of people dutifully performed a few decades ago upon arising, sometimes under the guidance of an instructor on the radio or on a record—and, indeed, that some people still do. Such calisthenics can ease muscular kinks, but more fundamental benefits seem to have been ruled out by competition among the originators of the systems to see who could come up with the easiest program. The ideal appeared to be exercise that required no effort, and some of the systems came close.

Dr. Latson, the critic of the physical culture professors, asserted that a great advantage of his own gentle twists and turns was that "they require practically no effort of body or mind." In 1907 Sanford Bennett, an elderly eccentric from San Francisco, published *Exercising in Bed*. The book is exactly what the title indicates, a manual of exercises that can be done in bed, alone, without even throwing off the covers. "I believe that muscles develop . . . more rapidly under these comfortable conditions than in the cold, bracing air usually advocated for physical exercise," explained Bennett.

The experts also vied to see who could devise the shortest exercise routines. Bernarr Macfadden had advocated working out as much as an hour a day, but in 1905 J. P. Müller, a Dane, began promoting *My System*—"15 Minutes' Work a Day for Health's Sake"—in America. Within a few years, however, competitors offered systems even less time-consuming, and so in 1924 Müller issued a revised version of his book called *The Daily Five Minutes*. Then somebody undercut this with a sure-fire four-minute program.

The most popular exercises in the 1920's were Walter

The date of this school-gymnasium scene is unknown, but the amplitude of the bloomers as well as the posture of the young ladies suggests the turn of the century. Clearly, if they had to get involved with dumbbells, they were going to do it as elegantly as possible.

The bewildering Indian-club exercise diagram, left, indicates a more forthright approach, although it dates from forty or fifty years earlier.

ABOVE: CULVER PICTURES; LEFT: BETTMANN ARCHIVE

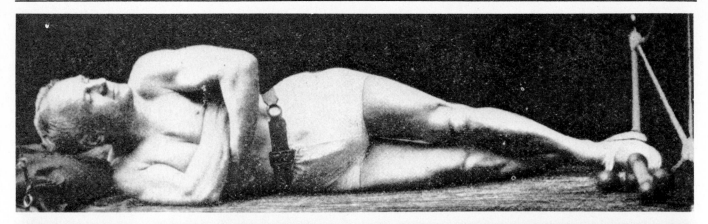

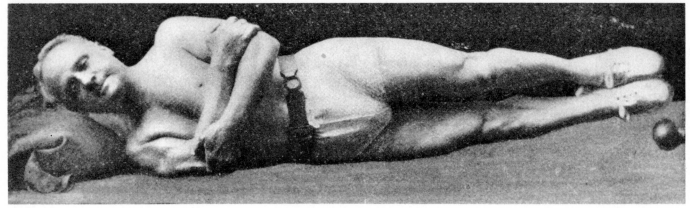

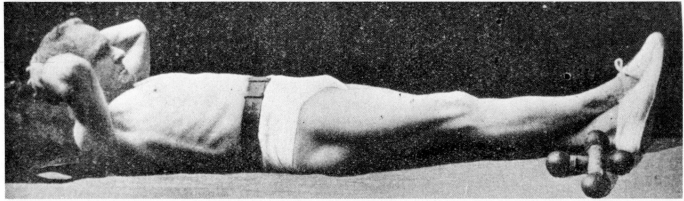

The ultimate in a laid-back attitude toward exercise was reached in 1907 by Sanford Bennett, whose book Exercising in Bed *was illustrated by instructional pictures like those above. Exercise, Bennett coolly explained, need not be uncomfortable. From the start, the impression has persisted that the proper equipment would make exercise not only effective but also easy. At the right is Spalding's 1896 model of an elastic body-building "instrument."*

Camp's Daily Dozen. Camp, a robust former Yale football star and the inventor of the All-American team, said he got the inspiration for his system by watching lions stretch at the Bronx Zoo. He gave the movements in his ten-minute routine alliterative names—hands, hips, head; grind, grate, grasp; crawl, curl, crouch; wave, weave, wing. "The essential thing is to go slowly," he advised. A casual test shows that the Daily Dozen will not raise a drop of sweat on a desk-bound forty-seven-year-old writer. The exercises approximate what a moderately serious jogger might do to loosen up before starting *real* exercise.

Considering the modest investment of effort, the benefits claimed for such exercises were truly remarkable. Constipation and dyspepsia, which seem to have afflicted people back then more than they do now, would vanish. So would sluggish livers, following a few repetitions of the "liver squeezer," a widely prescribed exercise that involved lying on the back and drawing the knees up to the chin. This was said to wring out the liver like a sponge. Preoccupation with fat was frowned on. "A prejudice against fat amounting to an abhorrence ought to be condemned," wrote a Boston physician, Samuel Delano, in 1918. But if you did want to lose weight, it was no problem provided you conscientiously practiced the deep breathing that was part of most systems. "Deep, purposeful breathing in the open air prevents the accumulation of fat, as it acts like a pair of active bellows on a furnace fire," said William J. Cromie, an instructor of physical education at the University of Pennsylvania.

Now and then a voice from the past expresses ideas about exercise not too far removed from present theories. As far back as 1890, a physical culturist named Edwin Checkley came out in favor of running, although he added sadly: "When I run for a few streets on a city thoroughfare, the populace look after me as if I were a 'freak,' or as if I were making off with something not belonging to me. . . ." Perhaps that explains why another pioneer jogger, Theodore Roosevelt, sometimes did his running at night while President, going out from the White House and trotting around the Washington Monument. Among medical men, Dudley A. Sargent, who directed physical education at Harvard from 1879 to 1919, sounded much like physicians today. Sustained, vigorous exertion that stimulates the heart and lungs strengthens the vital systems, he preached.

But where those of middle age or older were concerned, Sargent and the other exercise specialists who agreed with him generally cautioned against really strenuous workouts of the sort their theories seemed to require, such as long runs. Some of the authorities said that "gentle" running was safe, but they really meant "gentle." C. Ward Crampton of New York, one of the first physicians to sound the alarm over the mounting number of heart attacks among Americans, insisted that the focus of exercise should be to strengthen the heart and that running was well suited for this purpose. But, he said in 1924, sixty-four steps "is sufficient for anyone." That's a couple of laps around the living room.

At the time, even that would have been considered overdoing it in some circles. It was commonly believed that everyone was endowed with a fixed, limited supply of "vitality" and that strenuous exercise could lead to premature exhaustion of the supply, followed by invalidism or early death. A 1931 article on exercise in *Hygeia*, a

CONTINUED ON PAGE 12

The war effort in 1917–18 put great stress on physical fitness, even for stay-at-homes. At Yale, Walter Camp organized the Home Defense Guards for businessmen and Yale professors and put them through somewhat terpsichorean calisthenics every few days. In the photos above, ex-President and law professor William Howard Taft (front row, right) demonstrates amazing avoirdupoise.

BOTH: BROWN BROTHERS

Although Charles Atlas joined the other Greek gods in some Olympian heaven in 1972, the famous muscle-building mail-order course that he started in the twenties still flourishes; above is a recent version of his classic advertisement. Right: The "ninety-seven-pound weakling," as he was fond of describing himself in his ante-barbellum state, actually looked like this as a teen-ager, around 1910.

ALL: BY PERMISSION OF CHARLES ATLAS LTD.

Charles Atlas often started interviews by stripping off his shirt and sitting at his desk half-nude. His physique was his stock in trade, and he knew that people wanted a look. They got an eyeful: chest forty-seven inches; waist thirty-two; biceps seventeen.

Whether such splendor really sprang from the frame of a ninety-seven-pound weakling, as the pulp magazine ads for his mail-order muscle business proclaimed, is a fair question. Judging from a photograph taken when he was a teen-ager in Brooklyn, he was a fairly slender youngster, but no more so than a lot of growing boys. As the years passed, the man and the myth became increasingly muddled. Atlas' ads told the tale of the puny young man who had sand kicked in his face at the beach by a bully. Yes, Atlas sometimes said, a lifeguard had really done that to him at Coney Island, embarrassing him in front of his date, and it was this incident that had triggered his resolve to make himself so formidable no one would trifle with him again. But on other occasions he traced his determination to perfect his body to a visit to the Brooklyn Museum, where a huge statue of Hercules caught his eye. He credited a statue of Atlas—either at Coney Island or atop a local bank, depending on which day he was being interviewed—with inspiring his choice of a name when he became a professional muscleman.

He had been born Angelo Siciliano in southern Italy in 1892 and was brought to the United States by his parents at the age of eleven. Having developed his physique by diligent workouts at a YMCA gymnasium, he entered a competition sponsored by Bernarr Macfadden's Physical Culture magazine in 1922. He won and was awarded a thousand dollars and the title of "The World's Most Perfectly Developed Man." Capitalizing on the publicity, he dreamed up the Charles Atlas muscle-building course. The program consisted of thirteen lessons, brief pamphlets mailed out weekly, and it cost thirty dollars. In time, with the aid of an astute business manager named Charles P. Roman, he built a business that enrolled more than seventy thousand students a year, mainly young men. It continues to flourish today, even though Atlas died of a heart attack in 1972 at the age of eighty.

Atlas published the course in seven languages, and the ads featuring him wearing a loincloth and flexing his muscles drew disciples from all over the world. His organization still maintains an office in London besides its Manhattan headquarters, and at one time it had an office in Buenos Aires as well. In a 1942 interview with The New Yorker writer Robert Lewis Taylor, he claimed to have received a letter from India reading: "I've heard of the wonderful work you are doing and wonder if there is some way you can build me up. M. K. Gandhi." Atlas said he had sent along suggestions for diet—figs and prunes were among his favorite foods—and gentle exercises. "I didn't charge him a dime. I felt mighty sorry for him. The poor little chap, he's nothing but a bag of bones."

Atlas counseled clean living—no liquor or "secret habits"—but the heart of his muscle-building system was Dynamic Tension. This entails pitting one muscle against another—pushing the fist of one hand against the palm of the other, for example, or locking the hands behind the neck and pulling down while resisting with the neck muscles. There were skeptics who doubted that Atlas got the way he was from Dynamic Tension; "dynamic hooey," one rival muscle builder called it. Atlas himself acknowledged that he worked with bar bells, wall weights, and other apparatus before he discovered the secret of Dynamic Tension, and he continued to visit the Brooklyn YMCA for many years afterward. But there is something to Dynamic Tension. It is closely akin to the isometric exercises some athletes now use to increase muscular strength.

Atlas was not a big man—five feet ten inches and 180 pounds. But he was strong. To publicize a new roller bearing, he once harnessed himself to a 145,000-pound railroad car and pulled it 122 feet. He could bend railroad spikes double with his bare hands. On a visit to Sing Sing he bent iron bars as inmates watched intently. A number later wrote asking to sign up for the course. "I turned them down," Atlas said. "It might have resulted in a major break."

Atlas wasn't knotted and corded like a weightlifting body builder. Sculptors found him irresistible, and the landscape in New York and elsewhere is dotted with likenesses of Atlas' form—or portions of it—as the Dawn of Glory, Civic Virtue, George Washington, Alexander Hamilton, the Archer, Patriotism, Energy in Repose, and the forward part of a number of centaurs. Even when he was an old man, his once black hair gray, he turned heads at the beach.

For all his public flaunting of his body, Atlas led a sedate private life centering on his family. The Atlases spent their winters in Brooklyn and their summers in a house in a Long Island beach community, where Atlas trimmed his hedge and drove nails through two-inch boards with his hands at charity affairs. He conformed to the folk wisdom, dear to the hearts of all the ninety-seven-pound weaklings of the world, that the truly strong are gentle. Men he encountered would sometimes feel compelled to goad him to fight, but Atlas would turn away.

Not always, however. One day on the subway he suggested to a big bruiser who was sprawled over a couple of seats that he make room for a woman. As Atlas related it, the man demurred, saying "If you don't keep your face out of my business, I'm going to get up and knock all your teeth out." Atlas grabbed the man, lifted him well into the air, and gave him a good shaking. Thereupon the culprit recognized him—it would be nice to think it was the fellow who had kicked sand in his face many years before—and apologized. "I gave him a long talk about the value of physical exercise," Atlas recalled, "and as we waited to reach our stations he decided to buy the course." —P.L.

CONTINUED FROM PAGE 9

health magazine published for laymen by the American Medical Association, commented: "It seems that the more prodigiously we give of our vitality the sooner we exhaust it."

To buttress their case, exponents of this theory seized on every instance of an athlete dying young. Such deaths were not rare in those days; athletes, like nonathletes, could be struck down in their prime by infectious diseases since conquered by antibiotics. But the foes of strenuous exercise claimed in such cases that the athletes had squandered their vitality, weakening their hearts and their defenses against disease. Arthur A. McGovern, the proprietor of a gym in New York, kept a scrapbook of obituaries of athletes who had died by the age of forty, presumably to show clients who might be tempted to push themselves too hard.

McGovern and most of his fellow experts just about ruled out vigorous exercise of any type for anyone over forty. It went without saying that running was foolhardy, and the list of potentially perilous activities usually included bicycling, rowing, squash, handball, and tennis—even doubles. Warning of the dire fate in store for "those disciples of strenuosity," Dr. Delano of Boston offered fairly typical advice. "The heart and breathing are not to be unduly juggled," he asserted. Beware of the bicycle, which has produced "many a damaged heart and circulation." Tennis is risky because "in the volleying much *qui vive* and much holding of breath is necessary. It does the heart up easily—especially in the case of the nervous temperament." The only sport Delano wholeheartedly approved was golf. As for calisthenics, the doctor propounded his own thirty-four-movement system in *How Shall I Take Exercise and Set-Up?* Judging from the illustrations, for which the rather modestly muscled doctor himself posed somewhat sheepishly ("Let not the eye fall at once on the quantity of muscle. . . . For muscle by itself we have, as the reader must know, but scant respect"), the exercises consisted mainly of assorted grimaces.

If exercise was fraught with peril for men, it was even more so for women. Fielding Yost, who dispensed advice on exercise besides coaching football at the University of Michigan, said women should quit tennis at thirty-five. The idea of exercises to strengthen female muscles was absurd on its face. As Dr. Delano put it: "Femininity was plainly created not to have much muscle." The permissible exercises for the ladies in their middy tops and bloomers were mild in the extreme, with a trim waist and a "graceful carriage" the primary goals. An article by a woman doctor in the *Ladies' Home Journal* in 1907 reflected the tone that prevailed for decades. It recommended the exercise of touching the toes ("Austrian officers, who are noted for their tapering waists, make a special point of its use"). It also said that "healthy girls"—but apparently not adult women—could hazard stationary running in the bathroom, provided they started with no more than twenty-five steps and lay down for at least five minutes immediately after.

Clearly, even healthy girls couldn't tolerate much strain. Arthur McGovern, the gym proprietor, frowned on all strenuous competitive games for girls "as the element of excitement very easily leads to exertion injurious to the feminine physique." In a 1915 issue of the *Delineator*, Dr. B. Wallace Hamilton told the harrowing tale of fifteen-year-old Emily. She went off to boarding school, where she became nervous and jumpy from playing too much basketball. Hamilton prescribed a transfer to a school where the staff appreciated the frailty of young women, and a switch to golf and croquet.

If the theory that each person has a fixed stock of vitality is accepted as valid, then the logical conclusion must be that the wisest course is no exercise at all, and that is precisely the direction in which things moved. Whereas the electric horses that became popular in the early twenties demanded at least modest effort from the user, the abdominal massage machines that came into wide use a few years later required no exertion whatever. These machines, which whipped a broad belt back and forth on the user's stomach, supposedly stimulated the internal organs and dissolved fat, but by 1930 the American Medical Association, not always the most enlightened voice on the subject of exercise, felt compelled to state that they not only did no good but had caused some grievous injuries.

In 1925 a grim article entitled "Too Much Exercise" appeared in the *Saturday Evening Post*. Citing "overwhelming evidence that a great many Americans, of middle age or beyond, are exercising too much," it warned that any man over forty "who persists in putting unnecessary strains on his heart is fixing to make the acquaintance of the undertaker." The article ridiculed calisthenics and went on to question the safety of golf, which was just about the only sport left to doddering forty-year-olds by then. The stress and exertion of golf were vastly underrated, readers were told, and the nation's courses were more or less littered with the corpses of players who had collapsed from the strain.

The ultimate stand against exercise was taken by Peter Steincrohn, the doctor who dismissed all such activity as "bosh." In 1942 Steincrohn, a prolific writer on health topics, published a book that bore the alluring title *You Don't Have to Exercise* and the subtitle "*Rest Begins at Forty.*" It sounds like satire now, but it was dead serious. In fact, when the book came out, it was quoted approvingly by Dr. Morris Fishbein, editor of the *Journal of the American Medical Association*.

Steincrohn's thesis was that the heart needed rest, not

exercise, to stay healthy. Therefore, on reaching middle age it was best to avoid all exertion beyond that necessary for conducting the business of life. "Don't lift a finger unnecessarily after forty" was Steincrohn's motto. "Bending over to tie and untie your shoes; bringing the fork to your mouth; the rubdown after a shower; laughing; talking and reading—all these furnish your daily exercise requirements." Steincrohn, then in his forties, made clear that he had managed to shake the exercise habit completely, but for those who insisted on continuing to play a bit of golf, he advised dawdling on the course and taking a break for a smoke and a drink between nines. As for old codgers of fifty who persisted in playing tennis, he had nothing but reproach—"infantile exhibitionism."

Steincrohn reiterated his antiexercise arguments, only slightly hedged, in a 1968 book, but by then even he conceded that the tide of medical opinion had turned against him. A major force behind that change was Paul Dudley White, the cardiologist. In the 1930's White had become convinced that exercise to the point of pleasant fatigue—long bicycle rides were his favorite form— benefited the heart. When he came into the public eye after being summoned to treat President Dwight Eisenhower following his heart attack in 1955, White made use of his new prominence to promote the cause of exercise through speeches, articles, and interviews. Dr. White, who died in 1973 at the age of eighty-seven, was a dogged exerciser himself, pedaling his bicycle thirty miles a day even in his later years.

In the sixties and seventies White was joined in his crusade by many other physicians and medical researchers. Their central message was that the most valuable exercise for general health was activity that forced the respiratory and circulatory systems to work hard for prolonged periods. Far from draining the organism of vitality, such exercise was said to increase the efficiency of the heart and to expand its capability. The exercise needed to achieve this effect involves considerable effort; there is no such thing as effortless exercise. A typical program might call, for example, for jogging as long as an hour several times

a week, or perhaps for sustained stints of cycling or swimming. Most Americans still don't exercise much, of course, and many are still overweight, but, as the jogging craze in particular illustrates, millions have heeded the message. And their ranks include many well along in years. "Age is not a major obstacle to fitness," insists Dr. Kenneth H. Cooper. As the developer of the widely followed "aerobics" system, Cooper is more responsible than anyone else for starting Americans jogging.

It is conceivable that the new experts are wrong. But the assumption has to be that the march of medical science is generally onward and upward and that the exercise advocates know what they're talking about. Moreover, they are beginning to gather some statistical evidence that backs them up. A report issued in 1977 on a study of seventeen thousand men who enrolled at Harvard between 1916 and 1950 concluded that those who habitually exercised intensively suffered markedly fewer heart attacks than those who didn't. Similar reports are not yet available on women, and indeed one recent medical study of top women athletes such as Olympics trainees revealed the curious fact that a prolonged program of heavy exercise temporarily makes some women stop menstruating. There seems to be every reason to think, however, that the beneficial results of regular, energetic exercise are not confined to males.

Then, too, there is the subjective evidence of those who have found that they don't have to put aside games at forty and who derive deep satisfaction from the discovery that stamina can even grow with age. We are learning that we are not as delicate as was once thought and that we do not need to coddle ourselves, slow our step, and consign the tennis racket to the back of the closet shelf just because we are no longer young. In short, we are developing a whole new attitude toward growing old. And we can only feel sorry for all those who in the past were made to feel old before their time by the misguided fitness "experts" and the sedentary doctors.

☆ *Paul Lancaster is a freelance writer who works, runs, and plays tennis in Old Greenwich, Connecticut.*

A well-exercised Atlas rolls the globe— "Things move for men of mental and physical strength," proclaimed this advertisement for Kellogg's Grapenuts in 1911.

VOICES OF A VANISHED

AMOSKEAG

The life and death of the world's largest textile mill, in the words of the men and women who worked there

by Tamara Hareven and Randolph Langenbach

The sheer size of Amoskeag was staggering. The Manchester, New Hampshire, mills stretched along the Merrimack for over a mile on one side and half a mile on the other. The panorama above was made from the top of a 265-foot mill chimney in 1883, and shows both part of the mills and block upon block of company tenements. The weaving room (left) housed one thousand looms, just a fraction of the intricate, clattering machinery that spun out fifty miles of cloth each hour at Amoskeag.

Labor history is too often told in one of two equally unsatisfactory ways—in the icy language of economics, or in the fiery rhetoric of ideologues. Either way, the real people get overlooked. The story of the mighty Amoskeag textile mills at Manchester, New Hampshire, for example, is most often seen simply as a textbook case of industrial paternalism trying to outlive its time. The bare facts are simple enough, certainly. In 1837 the Amoskeag Manufacturing Company bought a fifteen-thousand-acre plot along the canal that bypassed Amoskeag Falls on the Merrimack and began to build an industrial town like the one its Boston-based founders had already established at Lowell, Massachusetts. The first workers were farm girls who eventually were displaced by successive generations of immigrants willing to work cheap—mostly Irish at first, then Germans, Swedes, Scots, French Canadians, and others. In the 1880's the corporation began implementing a master plan to create a model industrial city, and by 1915 Amoskeag was the world's largest textile center, with thirty major mills employing seventeen thousand men, women, and children. To keep their work force contented, the corporation provided a host of benefits—everything from a free cooking school to inexpensive housing. It all worked—so long as the textile business prospered.

But after World War I, the whole New England textile industry fell on hard times, thanks notably to competition from efficient, new plants located in the South, where labor came even cheaper. As profits fell, Amoskeag's management cut wages, extended hours, imposed speed-ups, fired or laid off workers. Strikes followed—the first in 1922, others in 1933 and 1934. In 1935 the corporation filed for bankruptcy and shut most of the mills for good. Manchester never fully recovered. Nor did the thousands of workers and their families who had known nothing but the Amoskeag life for three generations. Many of the mills and tenements have since been "renewed" out of existence (see David McCullough, "Epitaph for an American Landmark," AMERICAN HERITAGE, April, 1970), but some of the people who lived and worked in them survive, and now, thanks to *Amoskeag: Life and Work in an American Factory-City* by Tamara Hareven and Randolph Langenbach (to be published in November by Pantheon Books), their memories have been preserved to give us a sense, finally, of the people behind the Amoskeag story. The brief excerpts on the following pages were gleaned from the book. Like all authentic witnesses to history, these survivors defy easy classification: some are still fiercely proud of having been part of a great enterprise; others remember only the toil and the din and the bitter strikes; most seem to have mixed memories. But they all remember.

Workers in a burling room pause for a moment to have their picture taken, about 1910. It was their task to remove "burls," or tiny knots of wool, from new-made cloth.

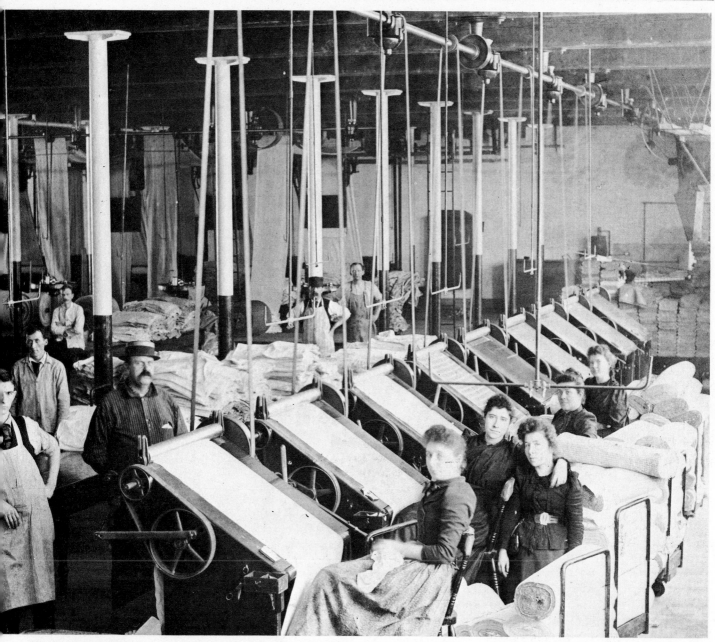

Raymond Dubois, millworker: *I was brought up in the area of the mill. All our people were mill people, and we didn't know anything else but mills. . . . We lived near the mills, we carried dinners for our parents, and we just were accustomed to the mills. It seemed like this was where we would fall in when we got old enough. I went in a few months after I became sixteen. There was an employment bureau run by a Michael Ahern. If you continually presented yourself in front of him, in the morning and at noon and at night, they'd finally get accustomed to seeing you. You couldn't become discouraged. There was a big line there going in for a job; and when a job popped up, and you happened to be the fellow in the line at the time, why, bingo! you got hired.*

Lottie Sargent, millworker: *My father worked most of his life in the cloth room. . . . It was fantastic to walk into. They had all different colors of toweling, and it traveled on rollers, all the way up. The whole ceiling, the whole room was just floating in cloth.*

Joseph Debski, management clerk: *Lots of times they complained that we hired too many Polish people or too many Greeks or too many French people. . . . We had a chart made up weekly, monthly, then yearly. It showed the percentage of all nationalities. Then if there were any complaints that we were hiring too many French or Irish or Polish or Greek workers, we'd compare them and find out what the variation was, and very seldom would it vary very*

much. The French [Canadian] people were probably 50 percent; the American people—like the Irish-Americans, Scotch, English—would run probably 20 to 25 percent; the Greek would run 10 percent; the Polish would run 10 percent; Italians we'd classify with "others."*

Ernest Anderson, millworker: *It was very seldom that you'd see anybody get to be a second hand or a foreman that didn't talk English. He had to be able to talk to the people and make them think that he knew more than they did. You looked up to a boss or somebody like that, even a loom fixer. . . . If you saw a loom fixer coming up the street, you tipped your hat to him—you felt he had made something of himself, that he was somebody.*

Alice LaCasse, millworker: *When I graduated from grammar school at fourteen, in 1930, I got a job in the mill. I was actually scared of the mills. As a child I used to go and visit my father in the spinning room. You can't hear yourself talk in there, the noise is so loud. So I was petrified when I found out I was going to work in the mills. My mother came with me to the office to get a job. We spoke to the man, and she told him that she preferred that I didn't work in one of the places where men and women were working together. She wanted me to go where there were only girls. So I got into the cloth room, where it was nice and quiet. It was all finished cloth. I was so happy there. I guess it was the relief of not having to go to those horrible mills that I hated so. When I would go to visit my father, I would almost cry.*

Yvonne Dionne, millworker: *I learned how to dance in No. 4 Mill, with the girls, not with men. At that time I didn't start work until eight o'clock in the morning because I was only sixteen. Those that were over sixteen started to work at seven o'clock. At noontime, the frames were stopped for an hour. We'd sit in the alley and eat our lunch; and if there was a good singer, she would sing and we would dance along the aisle.*

Thomas Smith, dyer: *The hardest job I had in the mills was when I was fourteen and took a job for the summer. It was a job I'll never forget, cleaning out the picker machines. All the cotton seeds that came out of the cotton would drop down under the pickers, and we would have to go under there and get all those seeds. We'd have a wad of cotton in our mouth to filter out the dust and keep us from choking. It would be so hot, and we'd get that cotton seed on our skin, and it would hit you something terrible. . . .*

Each of the mills had its own bell tower; and when the signal came over the electric wire, the bell ringers would jump onto the ropes. The ropes went up through all the floors to the bell tower, and all the bells would ring. When the bells rang, it was time to go home. The people flocked out of the mills. All the gates on Canal Street would be opened, and the people would come across the bridge. They'd be bustling and joking—nine thousand people trying to get out of those gates to get home as quickly as possible.

Whole families trooped off to the mills each morning, and children formed an important part of the work force. Lewis Hine photographed both the anonymous girl (opposite) and a solemn-looking boy named George Brown (left) on their way home at the end of a long work day in 1908. The oddly ornate machines the boys are pushing above are "broomless sweepers," used to gather up precious tufts of cotton from the spinning-room floor.

OPPOSITE AND LEFT: LIBRARY OF CONGRESS

*The company passed up few chances to
remind the workers of its beneficence.
Here, children play in the shadow of
the mill, about 1920.*

Dorothy Moore, bookkeeper: *I heard a woman say recently that the Amoskeag was such an awful place. Of course, it could be awful, because the mills themselves were terribly dirty, horribly dirty. But I was there in some of the better days of the mills when they were making a lot of money. It was wartime. Everything was looking up, so they did a lot for their help. For instance, they had a first-aid service, and they employed a doctor. After the mills went out, there was no doctor in town quite like him. Of course, any concern would have a first-aid station, where you could go with minor things, but the Amoskeag doctors would even come into your home. They had nurses who spent all of their time going around to homes where there was sickness. For their time the Amoskeag did all right, except in the way of money, perhaps. They didn't give much money. Now Jack Frazier, my husband's brother-in-law, has a very good job in the mills, but he was brought here because he was a baseball pitcher, just like they bring people to college because they are good players. Exactly! He was Amoskeag's star pitcher.*

Raymond Dubois, millworker: *People who went to work at the Amoskeag worked there until they died or until they got too old to work. Some lived in the corporation tenements. To live in them, you had to work in the Amoskeag. A son would move in with the father; and when his father died, the children would take over the tenement. In fact, a fellow told me one day that if he could buy all the real estate here, he would buy those tenements because they would never be empty. The people in the tenements had excellent living conditions. They all had a good roof over their head—it didn't leak—and they had modern conveniences, felt just like a millionaire—we didn't have to run outside.*

William Moul, weaver: *It seemed like you were locked in when the Amoskeag owned the mills. If you told the boss to go to hell, you might as well move out of the city. The boss had the power to blackball you for the rest of your days. The only way you could get a job there again was if you disguised yourself. Some of them did that. They would wear glasses, grow a mustache, change their name. . . . It was that or starve to death.*

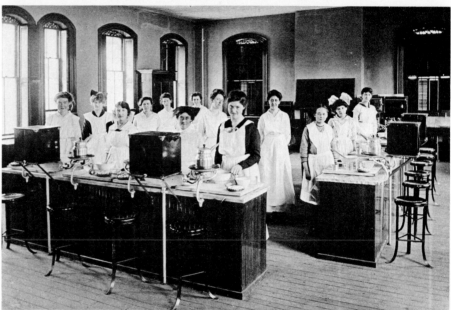

The Amoskeag baseball team (top) gave young men something to cheer about after hours. Young ladies could attend cooking class (above) in the Amoskeag Domestic Science School.

When Amoskeag's first strike began in 1922 (opposite), an era of industrial paternalism came to an abrupt end. One stern symbol of that system was treasurer F. C. Dumaine (top), who ran the mills out of the company's Boston office. The on-the-scene representative with whom the strikers had to deal was William Parker Straw, shown with his wife in calmer times (above) on the shady porch of the agent's house at Amoskeag. He had succeeded his father and grandfather as agent, and some workers believed the Straws somehow owned the mills.

Cora Pellerin, millworker: *When the union people came to Manchester, it was up to us to vote whether we wanted them in or not. [Treasurer F. C.] Dumaine himself said in a meeting that "the grass will grow on Elm Street before the union will come into my mill. I'll close it down." He said, "I've always been fair to my help, and I don't need the union. They have a union in Massachusetts, and they don't do what I do for my help." It was true in a way. It was on his account that we had all the benefits the Amoskeag gave us. Nobody else would do that, but the newer generation wanted more money, and they wanted someone to represent them.*

Marie Anne Senechal, weaver: *They put me out of the Amoskeag because I was talking for the union. After the strike of 1922, they made a company union, and I was elected to go to the meetings. There were about ten or eleven of us who went to those meetings, and they said we had to go back and tell our weavers that their pay was going to be cut. Get on a chair there and tell them, "Boys and girls, you've got to work for $11.00 or $15.00 a week." I came back and told the people what was really going on at those meetings. The boss, Bert Molloy, didn't like it. I was telling the workers what to do. So he said, "I'm going to get rid of her." It wasn't fair. . . .*
My father got fired once at Amoskeag. He had made a mistake in the cloth, and my father said to the boss, "The hell with you," and walked out on him. The next day the boss said to me, "Tell your father to come back in." So this was a really good boss.

Yvonne Dionne, millworker: *When I was little [my mother] worked in the Amoskeag. She'd leave one of my sisters, who was twelve or thirteen, in charge of us; but my sister wouldn't stay in the house. She'd go outside to be with her friends. One day, I tried to reach the kettle to take it off the stove, and I dropped it and burned myself and one of the babies. My mother never went back to the mills after that.*

Mary Dancause, millworker: *We had bad luck when they closed the Amoskeag. They did a foolish thing, wanting the eight hours. I'll never forget that. They closed all the mills. . . . People were never the same after that. I would never like to go back to those times.*

The interior of the Stark mill at Amoskeag, photographed the day before it was demolished in 1968

PHOTO BY RANDOLPH LANGENBACH

Raymond Dubois, millworker: *My mother was one of the few that didn't work in the mills after she was married. This was the reason my father worked so hard. I can remember my father working in the mill, seven days a week without a day off, without a vacation. He did that for seven years, without loafing one day. Would you believe that something like that could happen? Incidentally, when I say my father worked seven days a week, that included Thanksgiving, Christmas, and New Year's—seven days a week, 365 days a year. That guy had to go to heaven! He worked in the mill on Sundays. It's hard to believe. He worked from six in the morning till six at night, and I carried his dinners in. Then the hours got better; we went to forty hours. That eliminated a lot of this slavery, I'll tell you. He died at the age of fifty-eight. Of course, some people worked as hard as he did, and they lived to be ninety. I can't say the job killed him, but I can't say that it helped him either.*

Virginia Erskine, millworker: *Those were the good old days, when there was no pollution [laughs]. When I was a teen-ager, I lived in a corporation tenement on Canal Street, and the trains used to go right by, many trains every day. You could smell the carbon monoxide more than you can from automobiles now. But it wasn't just the trains; there were a lot of smokestacks, too. Most of the Amoskeag ran on coal-fed boilers. So there was a lot of smoke and pollution, but we didn't think of it as pollution. It was a livelihood.*

William Moul, weaver: *It's too bad to see so many beautiful buildings in ruins and to think that so many people earned their living there. Today, everything is falling down. If our old parents, who worked so much in these mills, if they'd come back today and see how these mills are, it would really break their hearts.*

Fidel Castro and top members of his revolutionary staff in the Sierra Maestra in 1957. Clockwise from Fidel are his brother, Raúl, kneeling; Guillermo García, a mountain guide; Dr. Ernesto (Che) Guevara, the Argentinian who became Fidel's closest adviser; and Universo Sánchez, his adjutant.

THE U.S. AND CASTRO, 1959-1962

Was the Cuban leader always a Marxist or did the United States impel him in that direction? A distinguished historian of Cuban affairs examines the critical years when the Castro revolution became a communist dictatorship.

by Hugh Thomas

One of the perplexing mysteries of the mid-twentieth century is why Cuba, a rich island with long and close ties to the United States, became a communist state. It did so in an unprecedented and unexpected way—without Soviet military help, without enduring a destructive civil war (deaths during Castro's revolution against Batista probably did not reach two thousand), and without the leadership of Cuba's Communist party, which played at best a minor role in such fighting as there was. By Latin American standards, Cuba, furthermore, was not economically backward. Indeed, in terms of per capita income, she was as wealthy as any country in Latin America except Venezuela and Argentina, and in some ways—as in her communications network—was more advanced and technologically sophisticated than Venezuela. She was, finally, as closely connected with the United States as it was possible to be without actually being part of the Union—the Cuban peso and the U.S. dollar, for instance, having been for many years interchangeable at par.

There was, to be sure, a dark side to life in Cuba before Castro. The political history of the island during the generations that followed the gaining of independence from Spain in 1898 had been characterized by electoral fraud, corruption, and bouts of tyranny. Political gangsterism had been rife. The economy had depended largely on the trade in sugar, which, while enriching many, left a large minority of the population chronically underemployed, unemployed, or destitute. Health and educational facilities were inadequate in Havana, the capital, and often nonexistent in the countryside. Neither the judiciary nor the civil service was free from political manipulation and intimidation. Relations between the whites and the black and mulatto minority were uneasy and became worse in the 1950's. The dictator of those latter years, Fulgencio Batista, indulged police brutality and military corruption and inefficiency. A typical story of Batista's last days concerns one of his communiqués, which announced that he was spending twelve hours a day with his generals, conducting the war against Castro. In fact, he and his commanders were whiling away the time playing canasta.

Partly because of adverse changes in the world sugar market and partly because of the growth, since the world depression, of strong, venal, and restrictionist trade unions, the country's economy had become stagnant. The unions frequently were charged with holding back the modernization of the sugar industry: Julio Lobo, the last great sugar merchant of old Cuba, for example, had a cane-cutting machine delayed at customs for two years and finally had to send it back to the United States. Though Cuba's previous history had been one of ready acceptance of technical innovations soon after their invention (Cuba had had a steam engine in 1798 and railways in 1833), the country, during the several years prior to Castro's accession to power, had become one of Latin America's least inviting prospects for foreign investment.

Still, such weaknesses do not necessarily make a country easy prey to communism. Venezuela had similar extremes of wealth and poverty in 1959. She relied more on oil for her stability than Cuba did on sugar, and she had less experience with democracy than Cuba had had. Yet when Pérez Jiménez, her last dictator, fell in 1958, the Venezuelan people were able to establish what became the most effective democracy in Latin America. A stagnant economy usually does not cause a revolution. Furthermore, the Communist party in Cuba was neither strong nor adventurous. Its middle-aged leaders did not seem unhappy about what appeared to be their remoteness from power. Communism in 1959, particularly after Khrushchev had explained the crimes of Stalin three years before, seemed a spent force.

Was it, perhaps, the United States that was responsible for what happened in Cuba in 1959 and subsequently? Since this view is widely held, it needs to be considered under two heads: first, the impact of the United States on Cuba during the sixty years between the Spanish-American War and Castro's revolution; and second, the interrelationship of the two countries during the second dictatorship of Batista (1952–1958) and the first two years of Castro's rule (1959–1960).

During the first third of the twentieth century, the United States dominated Cuba so thoroughly that the island was a U.S. protectorate in all but name. Prior to 1898, while the island was still a Spanish colony, the United States had become Cuba's most important trading partner and had

Puck's 1901 cartoon (above) declared that Cuba would be far better off as Uncle Sam's protégée than alone

Below: The crowd at Havana's Café Inglaterra in 1899—a curious mélange of planters, beggars, and U.S. military

invested some thirty million dollars in her economy. American intervention in the Cuban rebellion against Spain, from 1895 to 1898, led inexorably to the Spanish-American War, but in voting for that war, the U.S. Senate stipulated that it did not wish American occupation of Cuba after hostilities. Nevertheless, minds changed, and after the peace that secured Cuba's freedom from Spain, the United States insisted on three years of military occupation. Cuba became a nominally independent republic only in 1902. Even then, the Platt Amendment to the U.S. acceptance of Cuban independence, introduced by Republican Senator Orville Platt of Connecticut, gave the United States the right to intervene militarily in the island under certain circumstances: if civil war erupted on the island and if Cuba were not kept clean and free from dangerous disease. The Platt Amendment also placed restrictions on the Cuban government's capacity to incur debts and to embark on treaties with a third power, and enabled the United States to establish naval bases on the island—which it did at Guantánamo, to help secure the Panama Canal. These terms were as severe on Cuba as were those that the treaties of Versailles and St. Germain imposed on defeated Germany and Austria in 1919—and were as strongly resented.

A Cuban constituent assembly was prevailed upon to accept the Platt Amendment as part of the first constitution of "independent" Cuba. In 1906 the United States took advantage of its rights under the amendment, and another three years of occupation followed. The United States threatened to intervene again in both 1912 and 1917, each time with direct consequences to Cuba's internal political affairs. In the 1920's, General Enoch Crowder, the U.S. envoy to Havana, was given full powers to reorganize Cuba's finances, and in the same decade the United States recognized and supported General Gerardo Machado, even when he made himself a dictator. This support ended in 1933, when Sumner Welles, President Franklin D. Roosevelt's new ambassador to Cuba, helped inspire Machado's fall. The following year Welles assisted in the overthrow of a progressive Cuban government under Dr. Grau San Martín, which prepared the way for a new, only partially veiled tyranny under General Batista.

The Platt Amendment was abolished in 1934, but even so, the United States would not have hesitated to impose its own candidate on Cuba during World War II, had it been deemed necessary. It was not required: General Batista (who in 1940 was elected president—reasonably honestly) might have been a "son-of-a-bitch," but he was "our son-of-a-bitch," in FDR's words. Threats of U.S. intervention lasted longer. Probably the FBI knew of, and possibly may have encouraged, a plot to overthrow Dr. Grau San Martín in his second presidency in 1947.

The United States, meanwhile, had built up an economic position on the island as important as its political one. Investments in sugar mills gave U.S. companies control of 60 per cent of Cuban sugar production by the 1920's. American companies also had large landholdings. Cuban tobacco was marketed through U.S. merchants. U.S. companies, or their Cuban subsidiaries, controlled electricity, telephones, and other public utilities. Cuba was even sometimes represented in diplomacy affecting sugar by American citizens with Cuban interests. U.S. dominance over Cuban cultural life was almost equally strong.

Some benefits for Cuba naturally followed from this close relationship. Had it not been for American intervention in 1898, Cuba would not so soon have become free from Spain. The U.S. interest in Cuba raised the Cuban standard of living to half that of the United States by 1925. U.S. military doctors with the occupying forces made possible the conquest of yellow fever, for many generations the scourge of Havana (though it had been a Cuban of Scottish ancestry, Dr. Carlos Finlay, who first discovered that yellow fever is carried by mosquitoes). The building by a U.S. company of a railway along the length of the island was an achievement from which Cuba will always benefit. American investments in sugar mills were carried out with an iron determination to make profits and to ensure a supply of sugar for the United States in time of war, but those investments transformed the Cuban economy and gave it the shape that it now has. The close contacts established in North America by upper-class Cubans also meant that their children could easily be educated in the United States.

But this close association meant, too, that the United States was an all-too-useful scapegoat in Cuba when things went wrong. The United States habitually was blamed for the corruption of the elections, for the establishment of Machado's and Batista's dictatorships, for unemployment, and for poverty. From the Cuban point of view, U.S. behavior there was often characterized by a patronizing superiority toward local politicians, culture, and traditions, which was irritating even (or particularly) when it was justified. While many Americans went to Cuba believing that they were bringing prosperity, others took with them ideas of tax evasion, philistinism, and money grubbing. A substantial part of the quite large Cuban middle class became *dépaysé:* not only were people from that class educated in the United States, but they spent their years of exile, during the eras of dictatorship, in the United States, and even when preaching nationalism, Cuban politicians were often preparing their people to ask for a loan from the American government.

Cuban nationalism therefore, naturally, took an anti-American turn. The benefits which the Americans brought were easily forgotten. Cubans in 1898 argued that the United States had cheated them of victory over Spain; they attacked the Platt Amendment; and each new incident of intervention or threatened intervention created new waves of resentment. Historians at the University of Havana told students that each opportunity for national regeneration had been thwarted by "dollar diplomacy." It was into this tradition that Castro and the intellectuals of his generation were born.

The anti-Americanism of Cuban nationalist intellectuals burned strongly in the 1950's, though, by then, the Platt Amendment was long dead and U.S. economic domination of the country was much less notable than it had been twenty years before. But nationalists often dwell on past wrongs, and Sumner Welles's treatment of Dr. Grau San Martín was remembered as if it had happened only yesterday. (Grau San Martín, when he ultimately reached office, had abused his position scandalously to enrich himself and his friends, but he still represented in Cuba the memory of a revolution that the United States seemed to have betrayed in 1934.)

Thus, if one considers the sweep of Cuban history since the beginning of the century, the United States in a sense can be regarded as the unwitting author of the communist revolution in Cuba. The revolution was like a child's rage at a disliked guardian who had taken over in 1898 from the real parents, the Spaniards, after a war of ambiguous implications. But in the short term, during the years leading up to Castro's revolution, the United States played a much less obvious part.

The United States, as far as is known, was not involved in Batista's second *coup d'état* in 1952, but U.S. intelligence was active thereafter in Cuba. The CIA, for example, helped Batista set up an anticommunist agency in the Cuban government, the BRAC (*Buró Para Represión de las Actividades Comunistas*). "I was the father of the BRAC," Arthur Gardner, the U.S. Ambassador to Cuba from 1953 to 1957, told me in 1962. Also in the 1950's, Latin American radicals took notice of the CIA's involvement in a *coup d'état* that toppled Colonel Jacobo Arbenz's nationalist, but communist-supported, government in Guatemala. Che Guevara, the Argentinian who was subsequently one of Castro's most devoted followers, was in Guatemala at that time, and he obviously drew his own clear, harsh conclusions as to what the U.S. reaction might be to a new nationalist revolution elsewhere in Latin America or the Caribbean. Meanwhile Batista remained, till 1958, a favorite client of American businessmen and of many policymakers in Washington.

The attitude of the U.S. government toward Castro's movement against Batista was ambiguous at first. On the one hand, there were those officials who believed that Castro always had been a communist and should therefore be destroyed as soon as possible. This group included Ambassador Gardner; his successor, Earl T. Smith, who was ambassador from 1957 to 1959; and Admiral Arleigh Burke, the U.S. Chief of Naval Operations. Gardner suggested to Batista in 1957 that he should try to have Castro secretly murdered in the hills, where the civil war already had begun. Though Batista replied, "No, no, we couldn't do that, we're Cubans," there *was* at least one attempt on Castro in the Sierra Maestra, and presumably it was Batista's doing.

But many members of the American government took a different line: Roy Rubottom, Assistant Secretary of State for Latin American Affairs, had high hopes for Castro, as did the State Department's Director of the Office of Caribbean and Mexican Affairs, William Wieland. These friendly attitudes were shared by some officials within the CIA. Indeed, the second-ranking representative of the CIA in Havana had an open row with Ambassador Smith on the subject of whether Castro was, or was not, a communist, in 1957, and both J. C. King (Chief of Western Hemisphere Affairs of the CIA) and Lyman B. Kirkpatrick (Inspector General of the CIA) were, for a time, hopeful that Castro might turn out to be a liberal.

The United States thus presented a divided front toward Castro. He, in turn, was able to employ, to good effect, these divisions among both American policymakers and various molders of public opinion. A notable example was his use of the visit to Cuba of Herbert Matthews, a high-minded correspondent of the *New York Times*, in February, 1957. Castro saw Matthews in a remote part of the mountains and persuaded him that he was a moderate, nationalist reformer and that he had much more of a following than was really the case. Matthews' reporting was friendly to Castro and helped to create in the United States widespread sympathy for the rebellion. That sympathy, in March, 1958, enabled Rubottom and his friends in the State Department to ensure an embargo on the sale of arms to Cuba, an action as important for its psychological effect upon Batista as for its actual disservice to the Cuban army. Until then, Batista had assumed that the United States automatically would support him even if he used against his internal enemies American arms that had been supplied to him for "hemisphere defense."

By the end of 1958, Batista's position had begun to disintegrate, due largely to the corruption and inefficiency of his army rather than to the military skill of Castro—though it would be foolish to underestimate Castro's ability to make the most of a propaganda advantage in Cuba. The U.S. government made an attempt to get Batista to resign and hand over power to a junta of generals, which, in the words of the CIA's Kirkpatrick, seemed then to offer the United States "the best possibility of bringing peace" and avoiding "a blood bath." The task of trying to persuade Batista to agree to this plan was entrusted to William Pawley, an American with long-established business interest in Cuba (he had founded Cubana Airlines and was a personal friend of Batista's). Pawley's mission failed, possibly because Rubottom had told him to avoid saying that he was acting in the name of President Eisenhower. A week later, however, Ambassador Earl Smith, with the greatest personal reluctance, told Batista that the United States government judged he had no alternative save to leave, that the State Department thought he could now only be a hindrance to its hastily devised plans for a transition. Batista agreed, partly because he now had a great deal of money outside of Cuba, and partly because his heart was not in the fight, though he complained at the same time that the United States was carrying out still another act of intervention—and one which did, indeed, seem like a repetition of Sumner Welles's intervention in 1933 against Machado.

Before Batista finally left Cuba, one of his generals, Cantillo, tried to reach an armistice with Castro and even attempted to make himself the leader of a caretaker government. At the same time, the CIA was busy bribing the jailer of another officer, Colonel Ramón Barquín, a nationally respected enemy of Batista, to let him out of prison so he could assist in the formation of a new government. These and other last-minute plans all came to nothing. Batista's army was crumbling fast, and public enthusiasm for Castro and his allies was growing enormously, as Barquín and Cantillo in the end recognized. Batista left Cuba in the early morning hours of January 1, 1959. The U.S. government then realized that it had to choose between allowing Castro to take power and "sending in the Marines." The latter course was favored by Admiral Burke and probably by Allen Dulles, the Director of the CIA, but nothing was done. In the meantime, men and women from Castro's organization took over the maintenance of public order in the Cuban cities. Castro himself was in Havana by January 8, 1959. A new, progressive government was formed. In the beginning, Castro did not figure in this. Even when he did take over as prime minister, in February, the majority of the members of his government were well known to be liberals.

American reactions continued to be ambiguous, but in the Eisenhower administration those willing to give Castro the benefit of the doubt were predominant. The new ambassador to Havana, Philip Bonsal, concluded before arriving in Havana in February that "Castro was not a communist" and, at a meeting of the U.S. ambassadors in the Caribbean region on April 11, 1959, commented privately that Castro was a "terrific person, physically and mentally, he was far from crazy [and] he was not living on pills." Most press comment in the United States early in 1959 thought much the same.

There was, of course, some expressed hostility to the new Cuba in the United States, and Castro exploited it to strengthen his position with the reawakened Cuban public opinion. For example, when Senator Wayne Morse of Ore-

The American presence in Cuba has been uneven but never negligible since the Spanish-American War of 1898. One constant factor has been the U.S. naval base at Guantánamo Bay, a huge natural harbor near Cuba's eastern end. Captured from the Spaniards by American Marines aided by Cuban insurgents, the bay was to be rented "in perpetuity" from Cuba through an arrangement concluded by Theodore Roosevelt in 1903. Fidel Castro has denounced the American occupation regularly and refused the rent, but the Navy is still there. (The picture below, taken in 1927, shows most of the Atlantic fleet at rest at Guantánamo.) Various American diplomats have also played important roles in Cuba's internal affairs: the inset shows Sumner Welles, U.S. ambassador in 1933, who was instrumental in the fall of two Cuban regimes.

gon and various American newspapers and newsmagazines protested against the public trial of Batista's police, Castro suggested that their opposition constituted another variation on the theme of intervention. He also made the most of his visit to the United States in April, 1959, as the guest of the American Society of Newspaper Editors, to arouse further support for himself among the American people. Many Americans were even angry that President Eisenhower refused to meet him on that occasion, preferring to leave the task to Vice President Nixon.

The transition in Cuba from an open to a closed society, after that visit, came fast. In early 1959 Castro was still talking of the desirability of an "entirely democratic revolution." The Cuban revolution would be as "autochthonous as Cuban music," with no place for extremists or communists. In May, 1959, however, a classical agrarian reform, taking over large estates and giving land to squatters and peasants, was promulgated. This inspired a curt but polite U.S. note of protest, demanding compensation for all dispossessed landowners, Cuban and American alike. The reform caused a political upheaval in the countryside, though accounts of what happened are hard to find. Certainly it was then that the first resistance to Castro began to be organized by Cubans of the Right. Some politicians began to criticize Castro for failing to call elections. But Castro himself was busy directing abortive expeditions against the dictatorships in the Dominican Republic, Nicaragua, and Haiti.

In May, also, Castro dismissed several liberal ministers from his cabinet and had his first clash with the Cuban judiciary over a habeas corpus case. A month later the chief of the Cuban air force fled to the United States and told the Internal Security Subcommittee of the Senate that communism was beginning to take over in Cuba. A few weeks after that, in mid-July, Castro hounded out of office his own nominee as President of Cuba, Judge Manuel Urrutia, accusing him of treason and anticommunist expressions. Others who, like Hubert Matos, the military chief of the province of Camagüey, continued to criticize communism in public were shortly afterward arrested. Most of the other liberal cabinet members were then dismissed or were cowed into humiliating betrayals of their old faiths. The attitude of those who remained in office, like that of many liberals caught up in other revolutionary circumstances, is easy to condemn but important to judge objectively. The Cuban liberals who stayed with Castro in 1959 (like Raúl Roa, the Foreign Minister; Osvaldo Dorticós, President of Cuba for many years; Armando Hart, the Minister of Education; and Regino Boti, the Minister of Economics) were clearly men whose dedication to liberal ideology was not as firm as was their previously submerged desire for a strong nationalist state, which would break absolutely with a past in which none of them personally had been very successful.

Next, the truant former chief of Cuba's air force flew over Havana in a U.S. B-25 bomber converted to a cargo carrier, dropping pamphlets on the city. Antiaircraft guns fired at his plane, and some of their shell fragments fell to the ground and killed a few Cubans—an event that heralded a several months exchange of insults between Cuba and the United States. In February, 1960, only a year after Castro had taken power, Anastas Mikoyan, Deputy Premier of the Soviet Union, arrived in Havana to conclude the first commercial arrangement between Russia and Cuba, and in March, President Eisenhower gave his approval to the training of Cuban exiles by the CIA for a possible invasion of the island.

In the course of the first half of 1960, the independence of the judiciary, press, trade unions, and university was destroyed, and the flight of middle-class Cubans and liberals began in earnest. By then, a clash with the United States was inevitable.

In June, 1960, the Cubans asked U.S. oil refiners to process Russian, and not Venezuelan, oil. They refused. Castro retaliated by nationalizing the refineries. Eisenhower then cut off the U.S. sugar quota, an arrangement by which the United States bought a substantial portion of Cuba's sugar at a price higher than that of the world market. In return, Castro expropriated the U.S. sugar mills and all public utilities owned by the United States in Cuba. Eisenhower responded with a ban on all U.S. exports to Cuba, save medicines and some foodstuffs. The Cubans immediately took over all the remaining large private enterprises. In January, 1961, the U.S. embassy was withdrawn. Something like a new civil war had broken out by this time in the hills of Escambray in southern Cuba. In April the CIA's force of exiles landed at the Bay of Pigs. Immediately after the failure of that ill-starred invasion, Castro, on May 1, 1961, proclaimed Cuba a "socialist state" and decreed that there would be no more elections. The revolution, he announced, had given every Cuban a rifle, not a vote.

From this summary of events, despite the unfolding drama of 1960 and 1961, it will be seen that the real decisions concerning the direction the revolution would take were made in 1959, between May and October, and probably in June or July. Castro and Guevara on separate occasions mentioned that time as crucial, and it was then, also, that leading figures were first ousted or arrested for anticommunism. When the mere expression of anticommunism becomes a crime, it is a sure sign of what line a government wishes to pursue. By that time, the possibilities of achieving a humane or open regime in Cuba were over.

A proper interpretation of what happened, and why, must consider Castro's personality, first and foremost. Castro had a strong hold over Cuban opinion in 1959, and his position as "maximum leader" of the revolution was unquestioned. Marxism belittles the role of individuals in history. But in the establishment of regimes based on Marx's philosophy, individuals, from Lenin to Castro, have played decisive parts. Castro's motives, therefore, need to be investigated, so far as it is possible, in examining why the revolution in Cuba took the course it did.

Some would say that this question presents no real problems. Earl Smith, Arthur Gardner, and some others thought that Castro had been a communist for years. William Pawley claimed to have heard Castro, during riots in Bogotá in 1948, proclaim on the Colombian radio: "This is Fidel Castro from Cuba. This is a communist revolution. . . ." This interpretation of Castro's early loyalties has had corroboration from Castro himself. In a speech in Havana in December, 1961, he said that he had been an apprentice Marxist-Leninist for many years: "I absolutely believe in Marxism! Did I believe on 1 January [1959]? I believed on 1 January. . . ." More recently in a taped interview in Cuba with American television reporter Barbara Walters, in mid-1977, Castro said (though the section was excised from what was shown the U.S. viewing audience): "I became a communist before reading a single book by Marx, Engels, Lenin, or anyone. I became a communist by studying capitalist political economy. . . . When I was a law student in the third year at the University of Havana. . . . I became what could be called a utopian com-

Immediately after the success of Fidel Castro's revolution in 1959, many Americans felt favorably disposed toward him. He was a colorful figure in any case, and it was widely thought that he would bring democracy to Cuba. Visiting the United States at the invitation of the American Society of Newspaper Editors, he laid a wreath at the Lincoln Memorial in April, 1959. Something over a year later, in a pose that was a better weather vane of things to come, he was photographed at the United Nations embracing Nikita Khrushchev, the Soviet leader.

BOTH: WIDE WORLD

munist. Then I was introduced to Marxist literature. . . ." In another U.S. television interview, shown by CBS on June 10, 1977, he recalled his meeting with Vice President Nixon in April, 1959, and said that at the time, "I was a communist. I personally was a communist." In 1961, moreover, he had explained that if he had admitted in the Sierra Maestra how extreme his opinions really were, he would have been killed then and there.

Castro, therefore, had lent the support of his own authority to what may be described as a "conspiracy theory" in explanation of the Cuban revolution. Some other points can be added. For example, Fidel Castro's brother and intimate adviser, Raúl, had been an overt member of the Cuban Communist Youth Movement since 1953. Fidel Castro had influential communist friends at Havana University between 1945 and 1948, most of whom did well in the communist regime after 1961 (for instance, Lionel Soto, in 1976 Ambassador to London and an adviser on Cuba's African policy; Flavio Bravo, Deputy Prime Minister in 1977; and Alfredo Guevara, for years head of the Cuban Film Institute). Though perhaps not actually a member of the Communist party, much less a Soviet agent (as some members of the FBI suggested), Castro—so the conspiracy theory runs—must always have been in touch with the party.

When the communist leaders in Cuba realized that Castro was likely to win the war against Batista, they began to help him and accordingly were welcomed into the large alliance over which he presided, and which they attempted to take over from the moment that he and they arrived in Havana. Naturally (again, according to the conspiracy theory), Castro welcomed communist support, and this was why, save for making a few liberal gestures in early 1959, he failed to create an organized movement, with membership and branches, or to name a day for elections, or even to clarify the attitude of his revolution toward the democratic Constitution of 1940.

Such a conspiracy theory, however, does not really explain Castro satisfactorily. In 1961 he had good reason to want to assure the communists that he had been a Marxist for many years, since at that time he was being challenged by old-time Cuban communists like Aníbal Escalante. In 1977 he may have found it convenient to tell the world, and particularly the Third World, that he was a "utopian communist" in his university days, but at the same time, it is probable that he is not now averse to obscuring memories of exactly what he was doing at the university. Marxist or not, he was mixed up in the political gangsterism that stained the University of Havana at the time, and on a number of occasions between 1947 and 1949 he was implicated in murder charges. The Cuban Communist party in the 1940's and 1950's, moreover, was not an organization very attractive to a young man interested in power, and Castro was obviously that. Castro always believed in direct action, and the party's leaders were something of an early version of the sober, cautious Eurocommunists of the 1970's. In the mid-1950's, the public arguments between the Castroists and the communists over the desirability of an "armed struggle" did not sound like shadowboxing. The Communist party, it has been noted, did not play much of a part in the fight against Batista. Its leaders, indeed, were friendly with Batista's ministers, some of them having collaborated with Batista during World War II, even serving as ministers in his government. The head of the Cuban party dedicated a book to Batista's Minister of the Interior as late as 1956. The CIA thought that the Communist party numbered about

seventeen thousand in 1958, which would have made it the largest organized party in Cuba, but its electoral showing always had been dismal.

On the whole, it seems likely that Castro—whose speeches even today do not read as if they were being delivered by one who thinks much of Marx (there is scarcely a word of Marxist jargon in them)—wanted to found a radical, nationalist, populist movement which would embark on action, rather than join the passive and ineffective Communist party. Thus, the 26 July Movement (which was named for Castro's first blow against Batista, a raid on the Moncada barracks at Santiago de Cuba on July 26, 1958) grew quickly from its original few dozen, attracting idealists, fighters and opportunists, ex-political gangsters, as well as philanthropists. It no doubt always had the sympathy of some communists, but not of the party's leadership until 1958.

By the time Castro reached Havana, the 26 July Movement had grown to tens of thousands. No one will ever know how many there actually were in the movement, since no membership cards were ever issued: anyone could grow a beard and call himself a *fidelista* in early 1959. There was no congress of the movement, few officers, and no agreement on policy. Castro must have kept his eyes open toward the communists from the start, since Russia, the headquarters of the communist world, would be an alternative to the United States as a buyer of sugar and a supplier of arms. No doubt Raúl Castro, as a real communist, and Che Guevara, a long-time communist sympathizer, had been quick to point this out to Fidel. Even so, the thrust of the movement that Castro headed was in the beginning primarily nationalist and not communist, nor even particularly socialist. Castro told Rómulo Betancourt, the democratic President of Venezuela, in early 1959 that he was determined above all to have a row with the United States in order to purge Cuba of many past humiliations at the hands of the "monster of the north," as the United States had been termed by José Martí, the Cuban nationalist hero of the 1890's who was one of the chief inspirational figures of Castro's revolution.

In slightly different circumstances, in a different generation, with a different international posture by the world communist movement, Castro perhaps could have lurched as easily toward the Right, as toward the Left—say, toward Peronism or fascism. Fascist techniques were used so much during the early days of the Cuban revolution in 1959 and 1960 that, indeed, that useful term "fascist left" might have been coined to apply to it. Castro's cult of heroic leadership, of endless struggle, of exalted nationalism had characterized all fascist movements in Europe. The emotional oratory, the carefully staged mass meetings, the deliberate exacerbation of tension before the "leader" spoke, the banners, and the mob intimidation—all these Castroist techniques recalled the days of Nazism. Castro's movement gained its initial support less from the organized workers than from the same rootless petty bourgeois classes that supported fascism in Europe in the 1920's. As in Hitler's Germany, the workers joined the movement late, only after they saw that it was beginning to be successful and would be in power for a long time.

The temptation, however, for Castro to turn the movement toward communism must have been strong in 1959, since he knew that would be the course which would most infuriate the United States. It was risky to be sure, but he was, above all, the man for risks. As for the old communists, they had in their ranks, as Castro later put it to the *New York Times*'s Herbert Matthews, "men who were truly revolutionary, loyal, honest and trained. I needed them." Castro, no doubt, was surprised by the ease with which the old institutions collapsed before him. They did so because they had been compromised by their support of, or association with, the discredited Batista. Castro could not have known how feeble the liberal response would be, since his own movement had been built partly on liberal enthusiasm. But he did know that if he lost the liberals, he would require a disciplined bureaucracy in their place—"I need them." That was a true comment on Castro's association with the communists in 1959.

There is also another simple, but essential point to make: everything in Castro's past life suggested that if he were faced with having to choose between *fidelismo* (which would, in the end, imply adopting the rule of law and a risk of losing an election) and communism (which could give him an opportunity to remain in power for a long time), he would choose the latter. The brutality of communist regimes in practice never seemed to trouble him. In February, 1959, he made it perfectly clear that air force officers who had fought for Batista *had* to be found guilty of war crimes; a verdict of innocence, first returned, was rejected. Whatever hesitation Castro did display in 1959 was caused, surely, by anxiety lest an alliance with the communists might give power to them and their secretary-general, and not to himself. He needed to make certain that he could ride the tiger personally before he let it out of its cage. In this, he was showing himself primarily not the communist, but the Latin American *caudillo* that he really always has been.

Castro began to make use of the communists in the armed forces from the moment he arrived in Havana. Guevara made sure that the files of the BRAC, Batista's anticommunist police section, were seized immediately after victory. The BRAC's director was shot without a trial as soon as Castro's men reached the capital. A prominent communist, Armando Acosta, was made commander of the old fortress of La Punta in Havana as early as January 5, 1959—before Castro himself was in the city. Communist "instructors" moved into the army at once. Other communists were utilized from the start in the Institute of Agrarian Reform, which was established in May, 1959. By the end of that year, communists also were being appointed to ministries that were being abandoned by regular civil servants and *fidelistas*.

A careful study of available memoirs (those of Eisenhower, Lyman Kirkpatrick of the CIA, Ambassador Bonsal, and others), as well as testimony given to the Senate Internal Security Subcommittee in 1960–61 and to the Church Committee in 1975, provides no suggestion of any CIA or other U.S. action against Cuba during 1959. Of course, there was right-wing Cuban opposition to the Revolution, but the evidence is that the American government, the only serious enemy Castro had to face from then on, did not know how to deal with the apparently unique nationalist movement founded by Castro, and so did nothing the first year. The earliest material unearthed by the Church Committee concerning a U.S. interest in overthrowing Castro was a recommendation in December, 1959, by J. C. King, still the head of the Western Hemisphere Division of the CIA, to his chief, Allen Dulles, that, since a "far left" dictatorship existed in Cuba, "thorough consideration [should] be given to the elimination of Fidel Castro." The committee went on to report that the first discussion in the White House (among a

so-called special group of advisers) of any idea of a "covert program" to topple Castro occurred on January 13, 1960. There was some sabotage carried out in western Cuba by Cuban exiles in 1959, but the neglect in controlling such actions by Castro's enemies does not prove that there was a concerted effort by the U.S. government to overthrow Castro.

The dictator of the Dominican Republic, General Leonidas Trujillo, did launch an unsuccessful invasion of Cuba in the summer of 1959, but again there is no proof of any American involvement in that hopeless venture. When the ex-commander of the Cuban air force flew over Havana to drop pamphlets in October, 1959, Castro must have known perfectly well that the Cubans killed during the episode died from fragments of shells fired from the ground at the plane. But Castro described the flight as an attempt to "bomb" Cuba into submission, speaking, as Ambassador Bonsal accurately put it, "in a manner reminiscent of Hitler at his most hysterical. . . . There was the same blatant disregard for truth, the same pathological extremes of expression, gesticulation and movement." (Ambassador Bonsal's judgment of Castro thus had changed, as had the revolution itself, during 1959.) Evidence may yet be produced to prove that the CIA, the FBI, or some other agency of the U.S. government was active against Castro in 1959. But if it was, it is inconceivable that the activity was on a scale, or of a subtlety, adequate to divert a resourceful leader, such as Castro has since shown himself to be, from a chosen democratic course—from one, say, of re-establishing the Constitution of 1940. Cuba, or rather Castro, surely chose a path deliberately in 1959, and however much that path may have been determined by memory of old historical vendettas, it was certainly not affected one way or the other by current American policy.

The stability of the system that has continued since 1961 in Cuba is a contrast to the volatile days before 1959. Yet there have been curious developments. A revolution which once had as one of its chief aims the end of complete reliance on a sugar economy has laid emphasis on that crop more than ever before. The failure of the Cuban revolution to export its example to Latin America in the 1960's was, in the 1970's, compensated for by the dispatch of an expeditionary force to Africa. From providing the world before 1959 with sugar, cigars, and popular dances, Cuba, since the revolution, has provided it with *guerrilleros*. Cuba, at one remove, also gave President Nixon the hard core of disciplined "plumbers" who made Watergate. The Cuban connection with the stories associated with the murder of President Kennedy cannot quite be shaken off. Neither the far Left nor the far Right of U.S. politics would be what they are were it not for Cuba. This is a modern expression of an old U.S. tradition. Many will have forgotten that Cuba was an obsessive question in American politics in the decade before the Civil War. The Southern states' desire to increase the number of slave states by purchasing Cuba from Spain was indeed one of the causes of that struggle. During Cuba's two wars of independence, in the 1870's and 1890's, the island was a major problem in U.S. politics. It has been so once or twice in the twentieth century, too, never more so than between 1959 and 1962. Geography, as well as history, strongly suggests that she will one day play that part again.

☆ *Hugh Thomas, Professor of History at the University of Reading, England, is the author of* Cuba: The Pursuit of Freedom *(Harper & Row, 1971) and* The Spanish Civil War *(Harper & Row, 1977).*

A LEGACY OF HANDS

It has been nearly four generations now that these hands have been doing their work, bringing a special genius to an art form last seen on this planet two centuries before Coronado's expedition straggled into the American Southwest in 1542. The hands belong to Maria Martinez.

Maria lives in the Indian pueblo of San Ildefonso, New Mexico. She does not know her age with any precision, only that it is somewhere between ninety and one hundred years. What she does know with precision is pottery, clay taking on form and life under the movements of her hands. What she produces has been called art, but it is not an art that belongs to her time or to ours. It goes back to a people so far lost in memory that they emerge only as

by T. H. Watkins

shadows even in the long oral tradition of Indian history.

Call them the people of the thirteenth century, scraping out an arid existence in an arid land. They were not simple people. There are no simple people. In any given society of human beings, the anthropologists tell us, a certain amount of genius can be expected. Among preliterate peoples, that genius often expressed itself in art—functional art, more often than not, but art with as sure a sense of beauty as anything produced by larger societies.

So among these shadowy people of the thirteenth century there was art, left behind in the form of bits and pieces of pottery. In 1908 in Frijoles Canyon near San Ildefonso, an archaeological team headed by the Museum of New Mexico's Edgar Lee Hewett came across a scattering of shards. No ordinary prehistoric shards these: they shone black, unlike anything encountered in the American Southwest before. Already, young Maria Martinez had achieved local renown as a maker of pots, and Hewett sent for her at San Ildefonso and asked if she could re-create the kind of vessels from which the strange shards had come. She agreed to try.

The configuration of these pieces which had survived provided her with a clue to the shape of the original pots, and they were quickly reproduced. Giving the finished pots the odd black sheen of the ancient fragments was another matter. The shards held no clues here, but through patient experimentation Maria and her husband, Julian, finally contrived a solution. After each pot had been shaped and dried, Maria polished its surface with a smooth stone, a tedious and time-consuming job that produced a finish of remarkable clarity. The pots were then placed together in a pile, shielded with pieces of sheet metal so as to form a kind of ventilated oven, and layered over with—of all things—dry cow dung. The manure was put to the torch, and once the fire had taken hold, the whole pile was smothered in ash and additional manure so that the heat and smoke from the organically rich fuel could carbonize the surface of the pots. When they were finally pried out of the pile with sticks, the finished pots glowed with a black intensity that suggested Milton's description of the fires of hell: ". . . dark with exceeding bright."

Over the next several years, Maria and her husband refined the process, ultimately adding to it painted designs taken from the traditions of their tribe, the Tewas. The pots became famous—and expensive—and are now displayed proudly in museums and private collections all over the world. Maria and Julian, too, became famous. They found themselves and their work in demand at galleries, museums, fairs, and exhibitions; Maria herself laid the cornerstone for New York's Rockefeller Center in 1933. Yet in spite of more fame and fortune than had ever come to any member of the Tewa tribe, they lived as they always had lived at San Ildefonso, producing pots and children.

Julian died in 1943, but Maria continues to practice their art. Even more importantly, she has given her knowledge to her children, her grandchildren, and most recently her great-grandchildren. She hopes that when the time comes it will also be given to some of her great-great-grandchildren, thirty-two of whom have now been born. In any case, the art she rediscovered seventy years ago seems likely to survive. Maria herself believes it. "When I am gone," she once told her great-grandchildren (as quoted in Susan Peterson's recent book, *The Living Tradition of Maria Martinez*), "other people have my pots. But to you I leave my greatest achievement, which is the ability to do it." That is a legacy worth the treasuring: the hands of Maria Martinez have reached back across more than seven hundred years of history.

Nearly seventy years separate the work of the hands at left (1910) and that of the hands above (1977). In both photographs, the hands are those of Maria Martinez (seen opposite in a recent portrait), maker of pots, keeper of traditions.

LEFT: SOUTHWEST MUSEUM, LOS ANGELES; ABOVE: SUSAN PETERSON; OPPOSITE: JERRY JACKA

Original art by Brad Holland

"GOD...WOULD DESTROY THEM, AND GIVE THEIR COUNTRY TO ANOTHER PEOPLE..."

The mysterious diseases that nearly wiped out the Indians of New England were the work of the Christian God—or so both Pilgrims and Indians believed

by Alfred W. Crosby

In December of 1620, a group of English dissenters who "knew they were pilgrimes," in the words of William Bradford, stepped ashore on the southern coast of Massachusetts at the site of the Wampanoag Indian village of Pawtuxet. The village was empty, abandoned long enough for the grasses and weeds to have taken over the cornfields, but not long enough for the trees to have returned. The Pilgrims occupied the lonely place and called it Plymouth.

It was pestilence that had cleared the way for this tiny foothold in New England, and the shadow of death would be a major factor in giving the settlement form and substance in the months ahead.

New England Indians and European fishermen and traders had been in intermittent contact for a century, and it was inevitable that more than otter skins, beaver pelts, knives, and kettles would be exchanged. Disease was among the commodities, and in this trade the Indians would come off second best. Europe, with ancient contact by land and new ones by sea with the chief disease communities of the world, and with her relatively dense populations of often hungry and always filthy people, had all the advantages of her disadvantages: an arsenal of diseases.

Europe was in the midst of a golden age for infectious disease organisms, an era ushered in by the Black Death in the fourteenth century. To such old regulars as smallpox and consumption were added such new, or newly recognized, diseases as plague, typhus, and syphilis. Bubonic plague, the greatest killer of them all, smoldered continually and broke out periodically in consuming epidemics. Early in 1617 southeast gales drove whales ashore in the Netherlands. The fearful thought them a portent of plague, and sure enough, by August the plague was general throughout the land. London had full-scale epidemics of that killer in 1603 and again in 1625, and the plague—or something very like it—soon made its presence felt among the Indians of the Northeast coast of America. Innocent of immunity or experience, the Indians were helpless.

As Indian tempers rose, respect for Europeans fell in the second decade of the seventeenth century, particularly after the kidnaping of Indians for purposes of slavery began. Sometime in that period, a French ship was wrecked on the shores of Massachusetts, and some of the crew escaped alive. Possibly, in retaliation for a recent kidnaping

raid by whites, the Indians eventually killed all but three or four, whom they reduced to slavery. According to what the Indians told the Pilgrims, one of these captives, angry and helpless, had struck at his captors with words, telling them that "God was angry with them for their wickedness, and would destroy them, and give their country to another people, that should not live as beasts as they did but should be clothed. . . ." The Indians laughed at him, saying that they were so numerous that the white man's god could not kill them. He answered "that though they were never so many, God had many ways to destroy them that they knew not." Within a year or so an epidemic struck the coast of New England, devastating the tribes like an autumnal nor'easter raking leaves from the trees.

When did this pestilence first appear in New England? Probably no earlier than 1616 and no later than 1617, and it lasted until at least 1619. What vessel brought it? It is improbable that we will ever know. What was the disease? Another difficult question. We know it lasted through winters, which suggests that it wasn't a mosquito-borne disease, like yellow fever. We know that the few Europeans who actually saw its victims did not identify it as smallpox, measles, mumps, chicken pox, or any of Europe's common diseases, which they certainly would have recognized. We know it spread along the coast no farther southwest than Narragansett Bay, nor farther northeast than the Kennebec River or possibly Penobscot Bay, nor did it penetrate inland more than twenty or thirty miles. The narrow geographical limitations of the epidemic suggest that the disease was not one of the breath-borne maladies, like smallpox or measles, which normally surge across vast areas. A flea- or louse-borne disease like typhus or plague seems more likely.

We know that the disease produced spots on its victims' skins; and we know by hearsay that some Englishmen in New England at the peak of the epidemic slept in huts with dead and dying Indians, but that not one of these whites fell ill or even so much as "felt their heads to ache while they stayed there." Spots certainly suggest typhus. The Europeans' freedom from infection suggests some disease so common in Europe that they all had acquired immunity to it at home, or that they didn't stay around long enough to get a proper dose of the disease—or that the account is in part or whole false. Most of the seventeenth-century chroniclers called the disease the plague. "Plague" was and is a word often used to mean any pestilence, but these chroniclers often called it "*the plague.*" Captain Thomas Dermer, one of the few Europeans actually to see Indians who were freshly recovering from the experience, called their infection in 1619 "the Plague, for wee might perceive the sores of some that had escaped, who described the spots of such as usually died."

Plague is certainly capable of doing what this pestilence did, and Europeans certainly knew it well enough to recognize it by sight or description. And it is true that plague was well established in Western Europe in the early years of the seventeenth century. Like some kinds of typhus, it is a disease carried by rats and their attendant vermin, rats which swarmed in the holds of the sailing vessels of that era. The disease travels readily by ship, as the European colonists in America knew. Many Britons fell ill and died on the vessels of the Third Supply sailing to Virginia in 1609, and the rumor was that one of the vessels had plague on board. In the 1660's, during London's last great siege of plague, Virginians fled from their ports for fear of the disease coming across on the ships from England.

Fear was justified because ship rats were coming across and establishing beachheads in America. Captain John Smith tells us that they already numbered in the thousands in Jamestown in 1609, when the rats almost starved out the colony by eating its stores of food. They were present and prospering in New England by at least the 1660's, and probably a great deal earlier. It is likely that they found living in the layered bark walls of the Indian wigwams warm and comfortable, and the Indian food-storage practices and eating habits conducive to good diet. Once the rats were established, the transfer of their plague-ridden fleas to the Indians would have been almost automatic and perhaps not even noticed by the new hosts. Body lice were even more common among New England Indians than among white settlers, and the natives commonly passed the time by picking lice and killing them between their teeth.

It is disturbing, though, to those who diagnose the pestilence as plague, that Dermer described its chief signs as sores and spots, rather than the terrible buboes or boils of the groin and armpits that are impossible to overlook in typical victims of the plague. And it is even more odd that the plague-infected fleas did not establish themselves and their bacilli permanently among the wild rodents of New England, as they did in those of the western United States at the end of the nineteenth century. A diagnosis of typhus is tempting, but the historian is reluctant to contradict firsthand witnesses.

Whether plague or typhus, the disease went through the Indians like fire. Almost all the seventeenth-century writers say it killed nine of ten and even nineteen of twenty of the Indians it touched—an incredible mortality rate. But if it was, indeed, plague, it could well have killed that proportion. In the fourteenth century, plague killed one-third of all the people in Europe and a much higher percentage than that in many towns and districts. Further, the Indians knew nothing of the principle of contagion and had an ancient custom of visiting the sick, jamming into extremely hot little huts with them, assuring maximum dispersal of the illness. Their methods of treating illness, which usually featured a stay in a sweatbox, followed by immersion in the nearest cold pond or river, would have been a dreadful trauma for a person with a high fever, and a fine way to encourage pneumonic complications. Consider, too, that the epidemic could not have failed to disrupt food-procurement patterns, as women lay too ill to

tend the corn and the men too weak to hunt. Starvation often gleans what epidemic disease has missed. Consider, finally, that after the Indians realized the full extent of the disease, some of them, at least, ran away and left the sick and convalescent to die of neglect. In short, one does not necessarily have to accept a 90 per cent death rate for a given village or area in order to accept a 90 per cent depopulation rate.

It is undeniable that the pestilence largely emptied the Indian villages of coastal New England by 1619. That year, Thomas Dermer found "ancient plantations, not long since populous, now utterly void; in other places a remnant remains, but not free of sickness."

In 1621 a party of Pilgrims went to visit Massasoit, the most powerful Wampanoag sachem, at his summer quarters on a river about fifteen miles from Plymouth. They saw the remnants of many villages and former Indian cornfields along both sides of the river grown up in weeds higher than a man's head: "Thousands of men have lived there, which died in a great plague not long since: and pity it was and is to see so many goodly fields, and so well seated, without men to dress and manure the same."

Near Boston Bay, Thomas Morton saw even more vivid indications of the plague: "For in a place where many inhabited, there hath been but one left alive, to tell what became of the rest, the livinge being (as it seemed) not able to bury the dead, they were left for Crowes, kites and vermin to prey upon. And the bones and skulls upon the severall places of their habitations, made such a spectacle after my coming into those partes, that as I travailed in that Forrest, nere the Massachusets, it seemed to mee a new found Golgotha."

What destroyed Indian bodies also undermined Indian religion—the Indian's entire view of the universe and of himself. Disease was always considered a manifestation of spiritual influences, and the power of the powwows (medicine men) to direct and cure disease was central to the Indian religion. Later in the century we hear of powwows being hounded, punished, and even killed for failing to produce promised cures. What was the impact when hundreds, even thousands, died under the hands of leaders whose chief distinction was their ability to cure? Many of the powwows themselves, in constant contact with the sick they sought to cure, must have died. What was the impact of this final and irrevocable defeat of these priestly physicians?

What seemed cosmically appalling to the Indians was interpreted as clear proof of God's love by the Pilgrims—a divine intercession that revealed itself from the beginning. They had planned to settle in the Hudson River area or thereabouts, but the master of the *Mayflower* deposited them on the coast of New England. His inability or refusal to take them where they wanted to go proved a bit of luck—"God outshoots Satan oftentimes in his own bow"—for the lands about the Hudson's mouth, though more attractive because more fertile than Plymouth's, were "then abounding with a multitude of pernicious savages. . . ." God had directed the Pilgrims to a coast His plague had cleared of such savages: "whereby he made way for the carrying of his good purpose in promulgating his gospel. . . ." There were no Indians at Plymouth and none for eight or ten miles, and yet it had recently been a village of Wampanoags who had, over the years, cut away the tough climax growth of forest to plant corn. When the weak and hungry Colonists went out to plant in the following spring, all they had to do was to clear out the weeds. Death, it seemed obvious, was God's handyman and the Pilgrim's friend.

The wind of pestilence did more than merely clear a safe place for the Pilgrim to settle; in the long run, it enabled that settlement not only to survive, but to take root and, in the end, to prosper with a minimum of native resistance. The natives of coastal Massachusetts were fewer in number than in a very long time, possibly than in several thousand years, but there were still quite enough of them to wipe out the few Europeans from the *Mayflower*, and they had reason to hate whites. In addition to kidnapings, Europeans—English, the Indians told Dermer—recently had lured a number of Wampanoags on board their ship and had then "made great slaughter of them with their murderers [small ship's cannon]...." When a party of Pilgrims visited the next tribe to the south, the Nausets, in 1621, they met an old woman who broke "forth into great passion, weeping and crying excessively." She had lost three of her sons to kidnapers, and now was without comfort in her old age. A Wampanoag said that the Nausets had killed three English interlopers in the summer of 1620.

Half the English at Plymouth died of malnutrition, exhaustion, and exposure that first winter. Indian anger and Indian power could have made Plymouth one of the lost colonies, like the one Columbus left behind on La Española in 1493 or Sir Walter Raleigh's Roanoke colony of the 1580's.

At some time during this low ebb of Pilgrim history the powwows gathered in the fastnesses of a swamp, where, for three days, they "did curse and execrate" the newcomers to destroy them or drive them away. It almost worked: at times the number of English healthy enough to offer any real help to the sick and, if necessary, any real resistance to attackers was as low as six or seven. But in the end the Indians' gods failed, and the English survived, "having borne this affliction with much patience, being upheld by the Lord."

What held the Indians back from physical attack? They had the strength and motive, and bloody precedent had been set by both whites and Indians. The answer must be fear. The coastal Indians may have been second only to the Pilgrims in New England as believers in the power of the white man's god. A visitor to Plymouth in 1621 wrote that the plague had sapped Wampanoag courage, as well as the tribe's numbers: "their countenance is dejected, and they seem as a people affrighted." They were coming to the English settlement in great numbers every day, "and might in one hour have made a dispatch of us, yet such a fear was upon them, as that they never offered us the least injury in word or deed."

Direct relations between the Wampanoags and the Pilgrims began in March of 1621, approximately three months after the English arrival. An Indian walked out of the woods and through the fields and into Plymouth. He was Samoset, who spoke some English, having learned it from English fishermen on the coast of Maine. He asked for beer, and received "strong water," biscuit, butter, cheese, pudding, and a piece of duck. It was he who told the Pilgrims the old Indian name for their village and explained what had happened to its original inhabitants. A few days later he returned with the individual whom the Pilgrims would soon rank as "a special instrument sent of God for their good beyond their expectation." The man was Squanto, a Pawtuxet who had been kidnaped, had escaped in Spain, and had lived in Cornhill, London, before making his way back to America.

An hour later the sachem, Massasoit, walked in with a train of sixty men. If he had come to fight, he could have swept Plymouth out of existence, but he came in peace, and what amounts to a nonaggression and mutual defense pact was soon agreed upon—the Treaty of Plymouth. Massasoit, wrote Edward Winslow in his first-person account of that day in March, "hath a potent adversary, the Narrohigansets [Narragansets], that are at war with him, against whom he thinks we may be some strength to him, for our peeces are terrible unto them."

In the eyes of the native people of New England, the whites possessed a greater potency, a greater mana, than any Indian people. Nothing could be more immediately impressive than firearms, which made clouds of smoke and a sound like the nearest of thunderclaps and killed at a distance of many paces. And what could seem more logical but to see a similarity between the muskets and cannon, which reached out invisibly and tore bodies, and the plague, which reached out invisibly and corrupted bodies? In the 1580's, Indians in the vicinity of Roanoke had blamed the epidemic then raging on "invisible bullets" that the whites could shoot any distance desired; and it is quite likely that Massasoit and his followers had a similar interpretation of their experience with epidemic disease. No wonder the mighty sachem literally trembled as he sat beside the governor of Plymouth that day in March of 1621.

The following year, the Pilgrims learned that Squanto, taking advantage of his position as go-between for the Indians and English, had been telling the former that he had such control over the latter that he could persuade them to unleash the plague again, if he wished. He tried to use this claim of immense power to persuade the Wampanoags to shift their allegiance from Massasoit to himself. It was a game which nearly cost the schemer his life, and he had to spend the rest of his days living with the Pilgrims.

He told the Indians that the plague was buried under the storehouse in Plymouth, where, interestingly enough, the Pilgrims did have something buried: their reserve kegs of gunpowder. He told the Wampanoags that the English could send the plague forth to destroy whomever they wished, while not stirring a foot from home. When, in May of 1622, the Pilgrims dug up some of the gunpowder kegs, another Wampanoag, understandably disturbed, asked the English if they did, indeed, have the plague at their beck and call. The answer he got was as honest a one as could be expected from a seventeenth-century Christian: "No; but the God of the English has it in store, and could send it at his pleasure, to the destruction of his or our enemies." Not long after, Massasoit asked Governor William Bradford if "he would let out the plague to destroy the Sachem, and his men, who were his enemies, promising that he himself, and all his posterity, would be their everlasting friends, so great an opinion he had of the English."

Those enemies were the Narragansets, whose presence was the greatest immediate threat to Plymouth, and whose fear of the Englishmen's power was Plymouth's (and the Wampanoags') best shield. In the late fall of 1621 Canonicus, the Narragansets' greatest sachem, sent a bundle of arrows wrapped in a snakeskin to Squanto at Plymouth. Squanto was not present when they arrived, for which the messenger who brought the bundle was visibly thankful, and he departed "with all expedition." When Squanto returned and examined Canonicus' package, he explained that it signified a threat and a challenge to the new colony. The governor, who as a European of the Reformation era knew as much of threat and challenge as any Indian, stuffed the skin with gunpowder and shot, and sent it back to Canonicus. The great and terrible sachem refused to accept it, would not touch the powder and shot, nor suffer the bundle to remain in Narraganset country. The sinister package, "having been posted from place to place a long time, at length came whole back again." The plague perhaps had taught the Indian the principle of contagion.

Disease, real and imagined, remained a crucial element in English-Indian relations for at least the next two years, and seemingly always to the advantage of the English. In 1622 and 1623 the Pilgrims were still so incompetent at living in America that only the abundance of shellfish and corn obtained from the Indians kept them from starvation: a dangerous situation, because by then the Indians' fear of and respect for the whites were declining. As one Pilgrim chronicler put it, the Indians "began again to cast forth many insulting speeches, glorying in our weakness, and giving out how easy it would be ere long to cut us off. Now also Massassowat [Massasoit] seemed to frown on us, and neither came or sent to us as formerly." A letter arrived from Jamestown far to the south in Virginia telling of how the Indians had risen there, killing hundreds of the colonists. In the summer of 1622 a band of ne'er-do-well English settled at Wessagusset (Weymouth), not far from Plymouth, and after begging food from the impoverished Pilgrims, set about stealing it from the Indians. That fall Squanto, the almost indispensable man in the Pilgrims' dealings with the Indians, fell ill on a trip to collect corn from the natives. After fever and nosebleeds he died, asking the governor to pray for him "that he might go to the Englishman's God in heaven. . . ."

The Indians, apparently with the Massachusets tribe in the lead, began to plot to exterminate the Wessagusset settlement. They were less intolerant of the Plymouth than the Wessagusset people, but their plan was to destroy the Pilgrims, as well, for fear that the latter would take revenge for the murder of any English. The scheme never got beyond the talking stage. Why weren't the Indians able to organize themselves and take the action they planned? Pilgrims collecting corn from the Massachusets in the latter part of 1622 learned of a "great sickness" among them "not unlike the plague, if not the same." Soon after, Wampanoag women bringing corn to Plymouth were struck with a "great sickness," and the English were obliged to carry much of the corn home on their own backs.

Disease or, at least, bodily malfunction most dramatically affected New England history in 1623 when Massasoit developed a massive case of constipation. In March the news arrived in Plymouth that Massasoit was close to death and that a Dutch vessel had grounded on the sands right in front of his current home. The English knew of the Indian custom that any and all friends must visit the ill, especially the very ill, and they also wanted to meet with the stranded Dutch; so a small party set out from Plymouth for the sachem's sickbed. The Pilgrims found the Dutch afloat and gone, and Massasoit's dwelling jammed to bursting with well-wishers and powwows "making such a hellish noise, as it distempered us that were well, and therefore unlike to ease him that was sick."

Edward Winslow undertook the sachem's case and managed to get between his teeth "a confection of many comfortable conserves, on the point of my knife. . . ." He then washed out his patient's mouth, put him on a light diet, and soon his bowels were functioning again. The Englishman had, with the simplest of Hippocratic remedies, apparently saved the life of the most powerful man in the immediate environs of Plymouth. For the next day or so Winslow was kept busy going from one to another of the sachem's sick or allegedly sick followers, doling out smidgens of his confection and receiving "many joyful thanks." In an era which was, for the Indians, one of almost incomprehensible mortality, Winslow had succeeded where all the powwows had failed in thwarting the influences drawing Massasoit toward death. The English could not only persuade a profoundly malevolent god to kill, but also *not* to kill.

The most important immediate product of Massasoit's recovery was his gratitude. He revealed the details of the Indian plot against Wessagusset and Plymouth, a plot involving most of the larger tribes within two or three days travel of Plymouth, and even the Indians of Capawack (Martha's Vineyard). He said he had been asked to join when he was sick, but had refused for himself and his people. The Pilgrims probably had already heard rumors of the plot, and the sachem's story was confirmed by Phineas Pratt, one of the ne'er-do-wells from Wessagusset, who made his way by fleetness of foot and luck through hostile Indians to Plymouth.

Captain Miles Standish sailed to Boston Bay with a small group of armed men, tiny in number but gigantic in the power the Indians thought they possessed. They killed five or so of the alleged leaders of the plot and returned home with the head of one of them. The remnants of the Wessagusset colony were swept together and brought to Plymouth, where in time most of them made the decision to go back to Europe as hands on the vessels fishing along the Maine coast. The Indian head was set up at Plymouth fort as a visual aid to Indian education.

The Indian plan to wipe out the white colonies fell to pieces. Members of the several tribes within striking distance of Plymouth "forsook their houses, running to and fro like men distracted, living in swamps and other desert places, and so brought manifold diseases amongst themselves, whereof very many are dead. . . ." Ianough, sachem of the Massachusets, said "the God of the English was offended with them, and would destroy them in his anger. . . ." The Pilgrims noted smugly that the mortality rate among their opponents was, indeed, high, and "neither is there any likelihood it will easily cease; because through fear they set little or no corn, which is the staff of life, and without which they cannot long preserve health and strength."

By 1622 or so the very last cases of the plague had occurred in New England—if indeed these were examples of plague and not of misdiagnosis—and the only remains of the great pestilence were disarticulating bones lost in fallen walls of rotting bark that had once been homes. But it had done its work. In 1625 the Pilgrims, for the first time, raised enough corn to fill their own stomachs *and* trade with the Indians. The Pilgrims had survived and were getting stronger, thanks more to biology than religion, despite Pilgrim preconceptions, but Thomas Morton nevertheless was reminded of a line from Exodus: "By little and little (saith God of old to his people) will I drive them out from before thee; till thou be increased, and inherit the land."

☆ Alfred W. Crosby is professor of history at the University of Texas at Austin and author of The Columbian Exchange (Greenwood Press, 1972).

For further reading: The Invasion of America by Francis Jennings (University of North Carolina Press, 1975).

MRS. JACK AND HER BACK BAY PALAZZO

by Joseph J. Thorndike, Jr.

Today we would consider her eccentric; in her own time, many proper Bostonians thought that she was scandalous, but her friends were charmed by her free spirit. Henry James, for instance, once wrote to her, "I envy you, who always, even at your worst, loved the game, whatever it might be, and delighted in playing it." But regardless of any judgment about her character, there is no question that Mrs. Jack Gardner, shown at left in about 1905, bequeathed to America a unique treasure— Fenway Court. This excerpt from The Magnificent Builders and Their Dream Houses *by Joseph J. Thorndike, Jr., presents one of the book's enchanting stories of wealthy dreamers who were able to indulge their passion for building. The book, richly illustrated, is being published this month by American Heritage Publishing Company.*

One of Isabella Stewart Gardner's girlhood friends remembered a visit they made to the Poldi-Pezzoli palace in Milan when they were sixteen. Belle Stewart was enchanted by the Italian Renaissance paintings, the heavy carved furniture, the rich hangings, and ornate silver. "If I ever have any money of my own," she declared, "I am going to build a palace and fill it with beautiful things."

In later years, when she was Mrs. John Lowell Gardner, friends learned to take Belle's fancies seriously. "What Mrs. Jack wants," one of them said, "you can be pretty sure she is going to get."

Belle Stewart was the daughter of David Stewart, an enterprising New York businessman of recent fortune. At a finishing school in Paris she became a friend of Julia Gardner of Boston and, when they returned to America, was introduced to Julia's brother Jack. No one ever said that Belle Stewart was a beauty, but she had a magnetism that captivated Jack Gardner as it captivated many men (but few women) throughout her life.

In both fortune and social standing Jack was the heir of two Massachusetts families that had prospered in the China trade, the Gardners of Boston and, on his mother's side, the Peabodys of Salem. After he and Belle were married in 1860 he settled contentedly into the life of a proper Bostonian, looking after his investments, lunching and often dining at his clubs, fussing over the wines for dinner parties at their Beacon Street house, growing more staid and more portly with the years. He was also intelligent, industrious, affable, and, fortunately, tolerant.

Belle Gardner required a lot of tolerance. To the eagle eyes of Boston matrons her dresses always seemed to be fitted a little too tightly, the necks cut a little too low, the strings of pearls a little too long and showy. Where other ladies were content with a coachman, Belle drove out with two footmen on the box. The ladies found it unsettling when she once rode about with two lion cubs on the seat beside her. They professed shock when she invited them to tea in a drawing room where Sandow the Strong Man stood on exhibition behind a thin curtain, wearing only trunks— or, as some remembered, a fig leaf.

What scandalized Boston the most, however, as "Mrs. Jack" grew older, was her evident fondness for young men, usually young men connected with the arts. Whether any of Boston's suspicions were true is impossible to know, because if Mrs. Gardner bestowed favors she bestowed them on gentlemen, who did not talk. The evidence is limited to such appealing scenes as one that Ellery Sedgwick witnessed in the gymnasium of Groton School at a time when Mrs. Gardner was forty-eight and John Singer Sargent, the most fashionable painter of the day and her lifelong friend, was thirty-two. Sedgwick, later editor of the *Atlantic Monthly* but at that time a Groton undergraduate, was sitting behind some wrestling mats, reading *Ben Hur*, when "suddenly the gymnasium door was thrown wildly open and a woman's voice thrilled me with a little scream of mockery and triumph. Cautiously I peeked from my concealment and caught sight of a woman with the figure of a girl, her modish muslin skirt fluttering behind her as she danced through the doorway and flew across the floor, tossing over her shoulder some taunting paean of escape. But bare escape it seemed, for not a dozen feet behind her came her cavalier, white-flanneled, black-bearded, panting with laughter and pace. The pursuer was much younger than the pursued but that did not affect the

Some thirteen hundred persons are said to have crowded into Boston's sedate St. Botolph Club to see this likeness of the celebrated—or notorious—Mrs. Gardner by John Singer Sargent when it was briefly exhibited in 1888. Ellery Sedgwick was among many who admired this "beautiful portrait of her with her pearls roped around her waist, her beautiful arms glowing against a background that might have been the heart of a lotus."

ardor of the chase. The lady raced to the stairway leading to the running track above. Up she rushed, he after her. She reached the track and dashed round it, the ribbons of her belt standing straight out behind her. Her pursuer was visibly gaining. The gap narrowed. Nearer, nearer he drew, both hands outstretched to reach her waist. In *Ben-Hur* the chariot race was in full blast, but it was eclipsed. 'She's winning,' I thought. 'No, she's losing.' And then at the apex of my excitement, 'He has her!' But at that crucial moment there came over me the sickening sense that this show was not meant for spectators, that I was eavesdropping and, worse, that I would be caught at it. There was not one instant to lose. The window was open. Out I slipped and slithered to safety.

"For me that race was forever lost and forever won. The figures go flying motionless as on the frieze of the Grecian urn.

"What men or gods are these? What maidens loth?

"What mad pursuit? What struggle to escape?

"I knew not then whether it was lost or won. What I did know was that the Atalanta of that Sunday morning was Mrs. Jack Gardner and Melanion Mr. John S. Sargent."

Sargent and others who were inspired to immortalize Mrs. Jack in paint did not find it an easy task: she was a rather homely woman. But though her features were plain, she had some good points: sparkling eyes, fine arms and shoulders, and a magnificent presence. Sargent's best-known portrait of her, which hangs in the place of honor at Fenway Court, shows her standing regally in a plain black dress with a rope of pearls about her waist. The dress is tight and the neckline is cut a little lower than was the style of that day, but modern visitors to Fenway Court are usually at a loss to understand why the painting was regarded as so daring that her husband locked it up for his lifetime. The truth is that he had some provocation. John Lowell Gardner loved his wife, indulged her whims, and generally paid no attention to the gossip about her. But when the new Sargent painting was hung in an exhibition at one of his Boston clubs, some man made a remark that alluded, first, to the rumor of a previous affair with the writer F. Marion Crawford, and second, to a well-known geographical feature of the White Mountains. What the bounder said was, "Sargent has painted Mrs. Gardner all the way down to Crawford's Notch." It was when he heard of that remark that Gardner finally lost his temper and ordered the painting put away. Belle was unperturbed, although she did remark, when asked for a contribution to the Charitable Eye and Ear Infirmary, that she did not know there was a charitable eye or ear in Boston.

No matter how much they gossiped and carped at Mrs. Jack's behavior, proper Bostonians seldom refused her invitations. For she gathered into her circle not only the most brilliant of the talented young men but also the established intellectual luminaries of Boston and Cambridge. Among her closest friends and admirers were Henry and William James, Henry Adams, Charles Eliot Norton, James Russell Lowell, and Oliver Wendell Holmes. The literary lions were as dazzled as anyone else by Mrs. Jack, and more gifted than others in their elevated flattery. Henry Adams began a letter, "Wonderful Woman!" Henry James wrote: "I think of you as a figure on a wondrous cinquecento tapestry—and of myself as one of the small quaint accessory domestic animals, a harmless worm, or the rabbit who is very proud and happy to be in the same general composition with you."

If Boston's social matrons felt it necessary to keep an eyebrow perpetually raised at Mrs. Jack, other elements in the population were quite delighted by her. Their sense of propriety was not offended when, on a Sunday morning in Lent, she drove down to the Church of the Advent with a mop and bucket and did her penance by swabbing down the steps of the church. When her carriage was caught in a mob during some labor troubles in South Boston, a voice rang out, "Don't worry, Mrs. Jack. I'll see you get through." It was her friend John L. Sullivan, then heavyweight champion of the world.

Foreigners, understandably, were sometimes taken aback by her customs. Once, during a trip to Italy, she dispatched a handsome bouquet of yellow roses with her compliments to the king, Umberto. Unused to receiving presents from ladies, His Majesty sent an equerry to ascertain just what the lady's intentions were. It took not only her husband but also the U.S. ambassador to Italy to convince the court that Mrs. Jack was not an adventuress with designs on the king but simply an American who was accustomed to sending flowers to men she admired.

Mrs. Jack's male admirers, young and old, were of great help to her in what soon became the serious business of her life, the collection of great works of art. Sargent became her adviser on purchases, as did James Abbott McNeill Whistler, who had drawn a portrait sketch of her in London. Henry Adams found for her the magnificent stained-glass windows which may once have graced the abbey of Saint Denis. Henry James and others kept an eye out for noble English families that might be ready to part with the family treasures. Most important of all to Mrs. Jack was Bernard Berenson, whom she had taken up when he was a young fine-arts student at Harvard with long, curly hair and soft eyes. Berenson went on to become the world's leading authority on Italian Renaissance art and Mrs. Jack's adviser and agent for years.

At first the paintings were intended—or so she said—simply for her own house on Beacon Street. But they were purchased with a care and a sure judgment of quality that were seldom matched by buyers for the world's great museums. "I haven't enough money to buy second-rate things," she once said. "I can buy only the best."

Before she died Mrs. Jack had acquired the finest collection of Italian Renaissance paintings in the United States; it still ranks second only to that of the National Gallery, which received the collection of Andrew Mellon. Its single greatest treasure is Titian's *Rape of Europa*, bought through Berenson's skillful agency for twenty thousand pounds (then one hundred thousand dollars) from Lord Darnley. Rubens thought it the greatest picture in the world and painted a copy of it, which is now a treasure of the Prado in Madrid. Later Van Dyck, who had never seen the original, painted a copy of Rubens' copy, and Mrs. Jack bought *that*.

Perhaps the greatest bargain she ever got was Jan Vermeer's *The Concert*, one of only about thirty-six existing paintings by the Dutch master. When the picture came up for auction in Paris in 1892, both the Louvre and the National Gallery in London wanted it, but Mrs. Jack outbid them and got it for six thousand dollars. It was added to a collection that eventually included works by Rembrandt, Raphael, Botticelli, Piero della Francesca, Rubens, Simone Martini, and Mantegna.

In 1898 Jack Gardner died of a stroke at his club.

Between the inheritances from him and from her father, Belle found herself in possession of a fortune estimated at upwards of $5,000,000, sufficient to realize the ambition she had cherished since girlhood. Now she would build her palace.

During their travels in Europe the Gardners had been picking up not only paintings but bits and pieces of old houses, palaces, and monasteries. Among these trophies were the mosaic floor of the palace of the Empress Livia near Rome, a doorway and two stone lions from Florence, and eight balconies from the Ca' d'Oro, most resplendent of Venetian palazzi. All of these would be used in the palace she planned to erect on the newly filled land of Boston's Back Bay. Since the land had recently been salt marsh, the palace would have to rest on pilings, even as the palazzi of Venice itself did. The first pilings were driven in the summer of 1899.

Mrs. Gardner left the driving of the piles to the contractor while she took off on a final buying tour of Europe, but by spring of 1900 she was on the scene to supervise construction. First off, she decreed that the brick walls could not rest on a flat foundation but must be laid on an irregular surface of rough blocks so that they would seem to rise directly from the earth. Almost at once she ran into trouble with the building inspector in Boston, who insisted that such a large structure must have a steel frame. Mrs. Jack insisted that if marble columns would support a palace in Venice they would do so in Boston. At length, knowing that all of Boston was looking forward to seeing her "Eyetalian palace," she informed the inspector: "If Fenway Court is to be built at all, it will be built as *I* wish and not as *you* wish." As usual, she had her way.

During the next three years friends found Mrs. Jack a changed woman. Where she had spent money freely, she began saving pennies. The big rooms of her Beacon Street house were closed off in winter to save fuel, and guests accustomed to her lavish lunches found themselves facing a single lamb chop. Mrs. Jack had money for nothing but Fenway Court.

Although she employed an architect, Mrs. Jack was the true designer. She did not hesitate to turn window casements inside out, to put capitals of Roman columns under the columns they originally crowned, or to stick Victorian wooden tracery on a Renaissance wall. Thanks to her almost unerring taste, it all worked.

In fair weather and foul, it seemed that Mrs. Jack was always on the building site. She took her lunch with the workmen, bringing her sandwiches and contributing ten cents a day for oatmeal to clarify the drinking water. When the workmen had trouble getting the right pink-and-white effect on the walls of the courtyard, she seized two sponges and showed them how to slosh the paint on. On another occasion she wielded a broadax to demonstrate just how the timbers of the ceilings should be rough-cut in the old Italian style.

Among the Italian workmen who had been recruited for the job she took a liking to an ex-gondolier from Venice, one Theobaldo Travi, nicknamed "Bolgi," who impressed her as having the proper respect for the materials he worked with. Bolgi became her superintendent, and when Mrs. Jack found that he was also a cornet player, she worked out a series of signals for summoning the workmen she wanted: one toot for masons, two for steam fitters, and so on. Later, in her will, Mrs. Jack provided that Bolgi

More than half a century after her death, the courtyard of Mrs. Gardner's palazzo still precisely mirrors her eclectic caprice—just as she insisted it should. Her elaborate will made sure of that, stipulating that if any works "other than such as I . . . own or have contracted for at my death" were ever exhibited in the museum, the entire collection would go to "the President and Fellows of Harvard College in trust to sell"—in "Paris, France."

should be lifetime superintendent of Fenway Court.

During construction Mrs. Jack allowed only a handful of friends to take a coveted glimpse at the future palace, knowing that their reports would tantalize Boston society. Finally the palace was finished, and she sent out invitations to a grand opening.

If Fenway Court had collapsed, as the building inspector feared it would, on New Year's night, 1903, it would have wiped out virtually the entire social, financial, and governmental establishment of Boston. As the guests alighted from their carriages, they were ushered into the music room, at the far end of which Mrs. Jack had installed a horseshoe staircase. On the landing stood Mrs. Jack, triumphant in all her pearls, with two huge diamonds, the Rajah and the Light of India, swaying gently on golden springs set in her hair. Her guests, friend and foe alike, climbed up one side of the staircase, paid their respects to the hostess, and went down the other. To heighten the suspense, they were then treated to an hour-long concert by fifty musicians from the Boston Symphony Orchestra. Finally, at ten-thirty, the mirrored door to the courtyard was rolled back and the guests beheld the fairyland that Mrs. Jack had created. The pink walls, broken by the balustrades from the Ca' d'Oro, rose four stories to a glass roof. Here, in the midst of a bleak Massachusetts winter, was an enchanted garden of blooming flowers and tinkling fountains. Thousands of Japanese lanterns lit the courtyard and the art-filled rooms, still to be seen, that opened off it. Describing the reaction of the beholders, William James said that "it had a peculiar effect on the company, making them quiet and docile and self-forgetful and kind, as if they had become children" (although, as he added on second thought, children are just the reverse).

After her night of triumph Mrs. Gardner lived on at Fenway Court among her treasures for the twenty years that remained to her. After she had a stroke at seventy-nine she was carried about the palace in a Venetian gondola chair. Two years before she died, Sargent came again to paint the finest portrait of his old friend, by then a wraith, white of hair and skin and wrapped all in white clothing.

In her will she left Fenway Court to the public, with an endowment to keep it up and strict instructions not to change a thing. Fresh violets are placed each morning, as Mrs. Jack placed them, before Giorgione's *Christ Bearing the Cross*. Fenway Court neither lends its paintings to other museums nor borrows theirs for display. And even pictures that have been downgraded by changing taste or revised attribution hang where Mrs. Jack hung them. The strict provisions of the will have had one great compensating value: they have preserved Fenway Court not as simply a museum but as the home and creation of one remarkable woman. Thanks to the shrewd collaboration of Mrs. Gardner and Bernard Berenson, most of the important paintings are still recognized as the work of the greatest masters. In the history of art collecting there has hardly ever been a better investment. It is likely that a single painting—either the Titian or the Vermeer—would today bring at auction as much as Mrs. Jack paid for Fenway Court and everything in it. ☆

SAILORS, SHIPS & SEA TOWNS

Images of the Maritime West

by Roger R. Olmsted

Launching day: many of the Pacific lumber ships sprang right out of the woods that were the source of their commerce. The same Douglas fir that helped build the cities of the Pacific coast also turned out to be wonderful material for building sailing ships —from frames and keel through masts and decking. A band-saw, a gang of shipwrights, and a clearing on the shore equaled a shipyard in the unparalleled setting of the Pacific Northwest. The launch of the H. K. Hall (seen at the left, just about ready to slip down the ways into Puget Sound) was another triumph of Henry Knox Hall, who by the turn of the century was one of the last of the great American builders of wooden ships.

OVERLEAF: *Sailors called it Frisco: when you stood on the waterfront of San Francisco in the 1890's, you stood at the heart of one of the capital cities of the sea. And few scenes in any city in the world could match this image of San Francisco's Broadway Wharf with square-riggers drying sail amid the swirling steam and smoke of dockside donkey engines.*

ALL PHOTOS, UNLESS OTHERWISE NOTED, COURTESY THE SAN FRANCISCO MARITIME MUSEUM

Here is a bit of the old West nobody knows—or almost nobody—the West generally overlooked by both the fast-draw myth-makers and the scholars from the Land of Ivy. The cowpoke and the cardsharp, the sodbuster, the gunslinger, the prospector, the men who went down in the mines or up in the trees, ladies of the night and gentlemen of the road have all been popularized and exploited, analyzed and monographed. But scarce a word about poor Jack, who kept it all together out where the dust stopped short.

This is too bad, for there was both color and substance to his life. More men risked death at sea in the West than ever stood off Indian attacks; there was quite as much danger in reefing sail during a nor'wester as there was in descending the pit of a hard-rock mine; there was as much violence in a seaman's strike as there was in any range war; and the smell of salt spray makes for better romance than the taste of dust at the back end of a herd of cows.

And more wealth spilled out of the holds of Western sailing ships than was ever carved off the bones of Western cattle. Billions of board feet of lumber cut from dark, crowded forests and hauled out of Puget Sound and the tiny ports of California's northern coast. Fish, shimmering seas of fish, from the salmon and cod of the Alaska Banks to the sardines of Monterey Bay, cooked, canned, cartoned, and consumed throughout the world. Gold, silver, and copper going out; iron, steel, and coal coming in. Millions upon millions of tons of wheat loaded in the great grain ships out of San Francisco in the days when the monster farms of California fed much of the Western World. Millions of dollars invested in the vessels themselves, big and little—brigs, barkentines, lumber schooners, scow schooners, the tiny feluccas that harvested table fish, and the huge Yankee clippers that tied the West Coast to everyplace else. The industry that won the Far West did it to the beat of luffing sails.

Color and substance, but don't look to the television tube to find it; the myth machine rusted up when it hit salt air. Look here, instead, at these images, a handful drawn from thousands. They were made by amateurs and professionals, seagoing men and rank landlubbers, men known and unknown. They have been gathered and captioned by historian and former curator of the San Francisco Maritime Museum, Roger R. Olmsted, who has spent more than twenty-five years researching Western maritime photography. They are some of the finest documents that survive of a neglected glory—the golden era of the sea trades that served as the life lines of the farthest West in the days between the Gold Rush of 1849 and the end of the last and greatest age of sail.

A sea town made by ships: from the
rain forests of the north to the land of
sunshine in the south, the West Coast
lumber trade went all one way. When
the Southern California building boom
of the mid-1880's hit San Diego, this
second-best of California harbors was
a weekly stop—and in our view of the
steamer wharf at the right, four
lumber schooners represent the
significant activity: their cargoes are
helping to build a city that months
before was not much more than lines
upon a map.

The ships that slept: the quiet waters of San Francisco Bay's Oakland Creek (above) were a perfect place to lay up a ship for a season, or a year, or until freight rates took a turn for the better. In 1908, about the time this photograph was taken, a young seaman (later captain) named Fred Klebingat went over there looking for a job: "It was a grand sight," he remembered, "that forest of all kinds of rigs—ships, barks, and barkentines, brigs and schooners and steam schooners—a grand spectacle to one poetically inclined, but a depressing sight to a sailor without a job." Remarkably, when World War I sent freight rates soaring, many of the rotting derelicts seen here were fitted out and sent to sea again.

OVERLEAF: A schoonerman's holiday: in the 1870's and 1880's, one of the most important fixtures of a San Francisco Fourth of July was the annual regatta of the Master Mariners' Benevolent Association. Skippers of the lumber schooners would lay over for the opportunity to compete for the main prize—the right to fly the gamecock "Champion" banner for a year—and thousands of spectators would crowd the slopes of Telegraph Hill to watch vessels as large and cumbersome as barkentines being raced around a

yacht-club course more fit for a simple sloop. In spite of the size of the ships, the limits of the course, and the inevitably vast supplies of potables required for deckloads of holiday guests, the competitions were unmarred by any really serious disasters.

Rigs, lateen and square: out for salmon or halibut or anything else he can turn to market in San Francisco, an Italian fisherman plies the choppy bay in the 1890's (above). These exotic lateen-rigged boats provided the West Coast's most notable example of ethnic naval architecture; latter-day historians have called them "Italian Feluccas," but to sailors of the time they were "dago fish-boats." At the right, in a rare photograph of a square-rigger standing in under sail, the rust-streaked British Barfillan sails past Alcatraz Island at the end of a Cape Horn passage.

Square toes and reaches: above, on a nearly windless day, a towboat applies the "white-ash breeze" of its oars to move a deep-laden scow schooner the last yards to the San Francisco Hay Wharf. Until well after the turn of the century, these "square-toed" (flat-prowed), shallow-draft schooners catered to the city's gluttonous horse population, bringing hay down the creeks and river tributaries to the bay. At left, the lumber schooner Big River brings in another necessary commodity—redwood from the northern coast.

ABOVE: MORTON-WATERS CO., SAN FRANCISCO;
LEFT: OLIVER COLLECTION, BANCROFT LIBRARY

OVERLEAF: A trick at the helm: the man at the wheel in heavy weather has been a favorite—and often contrived—photographic subject for years. But there is nothing posed about this snapshot taken aboard an Alaska-bound square-rigger in 1925, when the great sailing fleet of the Alaska Packer's Association still made the annual run to the Gulf of Alaska.

A capital ship for an ocean trip: when the four-masted bark Lynton *visited Port Blakely, Washington, at the turn of the century, marine photographer William Hester sold the ship's crew an uncommon flock of portraits for the folks back home. Among them was one of the* Lynton's *captain, Lieutenant E. Gates-James (R.N.R.), seen above with his wife in their elegant quarters aboard ship. The* Lynton *was a veritable queen among the Cape Horn traders, particularly under Captain Gates-James, whose conception of "shipshape" staggered the imagination of a generation of shellbacks. Among other things, he required that mates were to wear uniforms and were not to be seen on deck with their coats off. "Ye Gods!" recalled A. Donaldson, second mate when Gates-James took over the ship, "after Capt. Thomas Gary Fraser, who considered a mate of no use unless he was covered with tar to his elbows, and had the tail of his shirt sticking out of the stern of his pants. . . ." A captain, however, was of no use unless he looked like a captain, and this Hester portrait (right) of one Captain Technor at the wheel of the ship* Parchim *in Puget Sound is a classic model—jovial enough, but not a master to be crossed.*

A capital crew for a capital ship: the wind was free and sailors cheap when the square-riggers still held their own on the twenty-thousand-mile route from the West Coast of America to Antwerp and London. Gotten by fair means or foul—shanghaied as often as not—the crews were cheap. And tough. Above, the mates and apprentices, the bosun and sailmaker, the carpenter and donkeymen of the ship Lynton may have posed for Hester while tenderly holding collie pups, kitten, and parrot, but we may be sure that they could crack a skull quite handily when necessary.

OVERLEAF: *Journey's end: one of the best-photographed marine disasters of the time was the colorful pileup of the British ship* Glenesslin *on the Oregon coast, October 1, 1913. It wasn't often that a square-rigger under full sail ran into a cliff in broad daylight; even rarer for the apprentice seamen to get a chance to pose right in front of the whole mess just after a dead stop on the rocks. The handsome* Glenesslin *was a total loss—one more entry in the long list of ships whose journeys came to an end on a dangerous coast.*

"CHIEF SATANTA, I PRESUME?"

Henry Morton Stanley, who later found Dr. Livingstone, reports the Treaty of Medicine Lodge, Kansas, October, 1867

In somewhat stiff repose, Henry M. Stanley sat for the study at right probably sometime in the 1880's— years after his reporting job on the southern Plains of America launched a career that sent him to New York, then to Africa, and finally to lasting renown.
LIBRARY OF CONGRESS

The middle months of 1867 were a summer of violence on the Plains. Above, Company K of the 5th Infantry beats off an attack by Cheyenne Indians near the Arkansas River on September 23. The painting was done by one of the battle's participants, private Hermann Stieffel, a German immigrant who spent twenty-four years in the Indian-fighting Army. More of his water colors appear on the following pages.

I n the summer of 1867, after more than a year of relative peace between Indians and whites, the southern Plains were in a shambles. It was an old story of blood and blunder by then. Consider this brief scenario: at dawn on November 29, 1864, Colonel John Chivington, 1st Colorado Cavalry, had led his men in a surprise attack on a sleeping camp of some seven hundred Cheyenne at Sand Creek, Colorado. At least one hundred and fifty Indians were killed that morning—and, according to a congressional report, killed with a feral intensity: "Fleeing women holding up their hands and praying for mercy were brutally shot down; infants were killed and scalped in derision; men were tortured and mutilated. . . ." Indian reprisals had followed in the spring and summer of 1865, and the military, depleted after the Civil War, could not control the situation.

Peace overtures were offered, and in October, 1865, United States commissioners met with representatives of the southern tribes—the Kiowas, Comanches, Kiowa-Apaches, Arapahoes, and Cheyenne—on the Little Arkansas River. Treaties were made, and peace, of a kind, settled on the Plains for the next year. But not in the uncertain heart of General Winfield Scott Hancock, commander of the Department of the Missouri. An occasional Indian "outrage" set his mind to whirling; furthermore, stories drifted around that the Indians were planning a major outbreak for the spring of 1867. In April of that year, determined to nip the supposed outbreak in the bud, he led a force of fourteen hundred west out of Fort Harker, Kansas, with the intention of showing the Indians "that the government is ready and able to punish them if they are hostile. . . ." The Indians were not intimidated; they met belligerence with belligerence, and, by the end of the summer, settlements and transportation lines were in a state of disruption. Once again, for all of Hancock's bristly declarations, the military was helpless; once again, a peace initiative seemed the only answer; once again, a commission was organized to treat with the Indians—this time at Medicine Lodge Creek, a tributary of the Arkansas River, in October, 1867.

On hand to write it up for the *Weekly Missouri Democrat* (St. Louis) was Henry Morton Stanley, a young man who already had made a bit of a name for himself as a roving

Company K of the 5th Infantry, Lieutenant Colonel David H. Brotherton commanding, was part of the military escort for the peace commission that met at Medicine Lodge Creek in October, 1867. So was Hermann Stieffel, who gave us this view of the commission's camp on the banks of the creek. In the distance, beyond the army tents and wagons, can be seen some of the 756 lodges of the various Indian tribes that came to deal and dicker for peace with the government. The scene at Medicine Lodge was not always as pacific as this. In his dispatches to the Weekly Missouri Democrat, Stanley reported one curious incident that took place near the end of the proceedings: "A few miserable Kaws, desirous of . . . capturing a few horses, made a raid. . . . Some Arapaho braves discovered them in the act of driving away their stock, upon which they gave instant pursuit. The Cheyenne Dog soldiers . . . galloped to the scene of action. . . . The Kiowas, the Camanches and the Apaches, urged on by curiosity, also

galloped up, until over fifteen hundred warriors were assembled. Imagine for one instant so large a body, dressed in the most fantastic manner ... riding the sinewy, fleet mustangs of the prairie, galloping in every direction. ... It was exciting in the extreme. Suffice it to state the Kaws were not killed, they were merely driven ignominiously away with a significant warning."

reporter. Born John Rowlands in Wales in 1841, he had emigrated to this country in 1859 after a childhood and youth made miserable by poverty and family rejection. A New Orleans merchant informally adopted him, and Stanley took the merchant's name as his own. During the Civil War, he served with the Confederates, then, after being captured, with the Federals. Footloose after the war, he started wandering—first to Denver and Salt Lake City, then to Asia Minor, penning letters and finally feature stories for various newspapers. In 1867 he was back in the West and had joined General Hancock's ineffectual show of force in the spring. Now he was with the peace commission, which, with an Army escort, a full press corps, and a gaggle of interested civilians, arrived at Medicine Lodge Creek on October 12.

They found waiting for them some five thousand Indians—not including a contingent of Cheyenne, who, with the stench of Sand Creek fresh in their memories, were waiting to come in until sure it was safe. "Monday morning about ten o'clock," Stanley wrote, "we came in sight of the great encampment of the Southern Indians. A natural basin, through which meandered Medicine Lodge creek ... was the place selected for their winter camp. The basin, hedged in by commanding elevations, was intersected by small undulating hills, deep ravines, pyramidical mounds. ... Thousands of ponies covered the adjacent hills, while in the valley grazed the cattle. ... All these camps were pitched so as to form a circle, in the center of which sported the boys and girls, and little papooses in a complete state of nudity. Thousands of warriors, braves, young bucks, papooses, damsels, and squaws, from the different villages, hurried up to satisfy their curiosity, viewing the commissioners. The escorts were all left to come on after us in an hour or so. This was a wise plan, as so many treacherous deeds have been done whenever the troops have come up, that the Indians have come to regard the whites as snakes."

A week later, the commission got down to business: "A vast amphitheatre had been cleared in the center of a grove of tall elms as the place where the grand council should be held. Logs had been arranged so as to seat the principal chiefs of the Southern Nations. Tables were erected for the accommodation of the various correspondents. Before these

At the right is Satanta, warrior chief of the Kiowas, whose oratory was famous among the Indians of the southern Plains. Stanley, too, was impressed: "By his defiant and independent bearing, he attracted all eyes. A solid chest, a large head, with busy, glittering orbs; fine ears, not too large; long, wavy shining black hair. . . . Agile and strong, he would certainly be a most formidable enemy to encounter alone on the prairie. . . ."
NATIONAL ARCHIVES

tables were the seats ranged in a semi-circle for the commissioners. Facing the commissioners were a few of the most select chiefs of the different tribes. Beyond all were the ponies of the chiefs, forming a splendid background...." The talking began, the government promising reservation land, food, equipment, and education in exchange for guarantees of peace, the Indian chiefs responding with resentment and resignation. The most belligerent was Satanta, warrior chief of the Kiowas. "I love the land and the buffalo, and will not part with any," Stanley reported Satanta as saying. "I hear a good deal of fine talk from these gentlemen, but they never do what they say. I don't want any of these medicine homes [schools] built in the country; I want the papooses brought up just exactly as I am.... I have heard that you intend to settle us on a reservation near the mountains. I don't want to settle there. I love to roam over the wide prairie and when I do it, I feel free and happy, but when we settle down, we grow pale and die.... A long time ago this land belonged to our fathers, but when I go up to the river I see a camp of soldiers, and they are cutting my wood down, or killing my buffalo. I don't like that, and when I see it my heart feels like bursting with sorrow." The talks continued the next day, when Satanta was terse to the point of insult: "The Kiowas have no more to say. We have spoken already. When you issue goods, give us all that is our due to us; do not hide any from us. Keep none back...."

He got the goods, as did the rest of the chiefs—but only after signing, with an eye on the coming winter, the requisite treaties. "Peace," Stanley wrote grandly, "has been concluded with all the Southern tribes. Civilization is now on the move, and westward the Star of Empire will again resume its march, unimpeded in the great work of progress."

Well, no. As it turned out, the summer of 1868 was no better than the summer of 1867; not for many years would permanent peace come to the southern Plains. Stanley himself fared better; his Medicine Lodge stories got him a job on James Gordon Bennett's New York *Herald*, and in 1871 the *Herald* sent him to Africa, where he stood before an aging missionary and, instead of reporting history, created it: "Doctor Livingstone, I presume?"—T.H.W.

Above is Stieffel's painting of the Grand Council of Medicine Lodge. At the left center of the picture are the U.S. commissioners. Satanta, standing to their right and characteristically hung with weapons, spoke. "I have no little lies hid about me," he said, among other things, "but I don't know how it is with the commissioners; are they as clear as I am?" Satanta signed the required treaty, but—like most of the Indian chiefs (and the government itself)—largely ignored its provisions. He ended up in the Texas state penitentiary, where he killed himself on October 11, 1878.

BIG GRIZZLY

The history of politics is a history of words. "Boss" is as American as "Santa Claus," both words being Dutch in origin. "Boss," wrote the English captain Thomas Hamilton, was a peculiar Americanism, a substitute for "master." Hamilton's book, *Men and Manners in America*, was published in 1831, roughly coincident with the rise of machine politics in the United States. It was during the 1830's, too, that "big" became a favorite Americanism, an adjective suggesting quality as well as quantity; power and prestige, not merely size. Yet it was not until after the Civil War, when the era of the big bosses was opening, that "boss" and "bossism" acquired a political significance. Most bosses ruled the swelling cities; a few perfected their machinery in order to run an entire state. Most were Democrats; a few were Republi-

cans. Many exercised a politically disputable, yet practically unchallengeable power over their local legislatures; a few were able to extend their power over their party in the United States Senate. Most had risen from the lower middle class; a few descended into politics from the upper classes. Most believed that power followed money; some believed money followed power. A few, having acquired power, wanted simply to hold on to it instead of parlaying it into something else—very different from the power brokers of today. Among these Boies Penrose of Pennsylvania stood out. Intellectually as well as physically, he was the biggest boss of his day.

His public life was an exaggerated representation of his times. He was born November 1, 1860, five days before Lincoln was elected President; when he

died, Wilson already had one foot in the grave. He was handsome and healthy in his youth; later he grew bloated and corpulent, like the Republic. Like the big engines, the big bankers, the gold watch chains, the national heavies, the solid citizens, Penrose looked, and in many ways was, a period piece. In other ways he was not. An exaggerated representation is not necessarily a caricature; and Penrose cared little for his image. He was loath to pay tribute to virtue. This, in an age marked by gross hypocrisy, was one of the more remarkable features of his character.

Childhood photographs of Boies Penrose show an extraordinarily beautiful child. Except for his clothes, and except for the inevitable atmosphere which such images breathe, there is nothing very Victorian

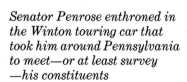
Senator Penrose enthroned in the Winton touring car that took him around Pennsylvania to meet—or at least survey —his constituents

Gargantuan, gross, and cynical, the patrician boss
Boies Penrose descended from aristocracy to dominate
Pennsylvania Republican politics for thirty years

by John Lukacs

about him. He has a Regency face, almost porcelain in its fineness: a remarkable forehead, clear strong eyes, a slightly pouting lower lip, an expression that is disdainful rather than contemptuous, rather English, and very different from his later senatorial countenance, which had something Germanic about it and not only because of his enormous bulk.

He was born an Anglo-American aristocrat. This word has been misused in recent times, promiscuously attributed to families who, no matter how successful and rich, are but one generation removed from the middle class. The founder of the family in America, Bartholomew Penrose, came from a Cornish family of a certain distinction. His son Thomas became a rich shipowner in colonial Philadelphia. His son married the daughter of a most promi-

nent Philadelphia family; his grandson married the granddaughter of a younger son of the Duke of Norfolk. The grandson of *this* grandson was Boies's father, Dr. Richard Alexander Fullerton Penrose, who married Sarah Hannah Boies—among whose ancestors were two graduates of the first Harvard College class in 1642; the secretary to Lord Baltimore; and the Earl of Charteris.

The portraits of Boies's father show a patrician, dignified, kind physician. His wife was lovely, learned, and strong. They were a handsome, intelligent, successful couple, yet they chose to withdraw from the greater world. Everything about their lives suggests a curious and melancholy reticence, an odd mixture of shyness and pride, a withdrawal into a kind of interior life, as if this were the only decent way to

live at the time of the booming blossoming of the American democracy. They lived at 1331 Spruce Street, in a comfortable house of small dimensions, few ornaments, and no pretensions. In the 1860's this house stood on the edge of the fashionable portion of the eighth ward of Philadelphia, most of the prominent and rich families having moved farther west, across Broad Street. The Penroses did not participate in this social migration. In spite of her great beauty and intelligence and family connections, Dr. Penrose's young wife showed little interest in society. She bore him seven sons within ten years.

Her two oldest sons, Boies and Charles Bingham, were tutored at home. They graduated from Episcopal Academy with equally high marks. Although fifteen months apart in age,

they entered Harvard University together. Here the parallel ends. While his brother advanced from honor to honor, Boies Penrose was on the verge of being expelled at the outset of his senior year. His parents were disturbed. Letters passed between Spruce Street and Cambridge. He learned that his mother was dying, and his purposeful character asserted itself. He rallied and graduated with honors, only to return from Boston to a house half-empty. His mother had died.

Between 1881, when Penrose returned from Harvard, and 1884, when he chose to enter politics, the city of Philadelphia underwent a political revolution: a complete turn of the wheel. Prominent citizens had roused themselves in the cause of reform. A Committee of One Hundred raised the banner against the corrupt Gas Ring which ruled City Hall. In 1881 they succeeded in electing a reform mayor and a reformist receiver of taxes. They did not succeed in reforming either the habits of the municipal bureaucracy or the voting habits of the electorate. In 1883 the voters rejected the reform controller; the next year, they turned the amiable reform mayor out of office. The machine was back in power. There were a few new faces among the leaders. The wheel had gone full circle: the Ring remained at the hub.

Boies Penrose was both witness and participant in these events. He saw the Gas Ring for what it was: artless and corrupt, shameless and vulgar. He was reading law in a firm whose senior partners were champions in the struggle for municipal regeneration, as was the senior partner of the firm Penrose would join when he was admitted to the bar. In the municipal election of February, 1884, the young Penrose stepped up to the battlements. He stood at the polling places, tall—six feet four—and defiant, sporting a large reform badge on his overcoat; he held a no less impressive copy of the Voters' Register in his hand. The toughs of the ward leaders growled and snapped around him, but to no avail. There were no tricks at the polls that day. In a ward which had been one of the safest for the machine, its candidate lost three to one. Everyone saw that this was due mostly to Penrose. He had intimidated the intimidators. He was the civic hero of the day.

It was a turning point in his life. The proper people of Philadelphia were impressed. So were the politicians and the ward leaders. There occurred now a marriage of convenience. Penrose was interested in politics; the politicians were interested in Penrose. The ward leaders did not merely take to him; they took to him on his terms. He wanted to be chosen for the state legislature; they nominated and elected him. On a raw January day in 1885 Penrose took the train to Harrisburg. His political career was launched.

Many people later suggested that this turning point had coincided with a transformation of his character. Penrose chose a career in politics at a time when Lord Bryce was asking "Why the Best Men Do Not Go into Politics." Yet the young patrician did not go in as a reformer; he became voracious, cynical, and impenitent. Penrose threw himself into the muddy pool of politics, the theory goes, because he liked low company. This may be too simple an explanation. Within the family there was a precedent. His grandfather, whose career he studied and admired, had been a politician. Charles Bingham Penrose, with his noble brow and his breathtakingly beautiful wife, had enjoyed the rude sounds and smells of the political arena. First state senator, then president of the Pennsylvania Senate, he had been instrumental in electing Simon Cameron, one of the most ruthless and corrupt politicians of the era, to the United States Senate in 1857; he was a close friend of Thaddeus Stevens; he was one of the founders of the Republican party in Philadelphia. He was largely indifferent to those proper Philadelphians who disapproved of him. He may have had a taste for low company; he certainly had an appetite for power.

His grandson Boies, too, believed in power; he thought in terms of it, as was evident from his earliest political writings. The contrast between the young patrician and the corrupt politician may be intellectually and logically attractive; but it will not stand. As a twenty-year-old Harvard student, Penrose had delivered an oration on "Martin Van Buren as a Politician." This terse, opinionated, and clear paper dealt with the origins of bossism; it also contained, in a nutshell, the lifelong political philosophy of Boies Penrose.

"Martin Van Buren," Penrose began, "was the first and the greatest of American politicians; of that class of statesmen who owe their success not so much to their opinions or characters, as to their skill in managing the machinery of party. . . . He marks the transition in American politics from statesmen like Adams and Webster to the great political bosses and managers of today. . . . Adams was the last statesman of the old school who was to occupy the White House, Van Buren was the first politician president." This was "the inevitable outcome" of the development of the country. "The voters of the United States were no longer the same voters who had founded the Constitution. In the rivalries of parties, the mechanical arts of electioneering were soon reduced to a system. . . . Political opinions, in fact, were a secondary consideration. All the statesmanship that the times required was the artful adaptation of general propositions to the existing temper and opinions of the masses.

"We can now understand the contempt which the practical politician bestows too often upon the civil service reformer. . . ." The preaching "by a certain class of political amateurs" amounts to little; it is often "peculiarly unjust. By management and not by statesmanship are questions generally decided in the Legislatures. . . . When management is all that is essential have we a right to be disappointed if Van Buren is not Webster?"

All of Penrose's political career was consistent with this conclusion.

The acuity of his mind was extraordinary. In spite of (or perhaps because of) his considerable learning, Penrose developed an early disdain for the presentations of the Harvard professorate. He was a vigorous youth, with powerful appetites, physical as well as mental. His father, who had an exaggerated conviction about the virtues of dieting, became ever more withdrawn. The young Boies went out, night after night, to oyster houses and steakhouses where he would sit, solitary and saturnine, downing large quantities of food and drink. During the day he was that most proper of Philadelphians, a young lawyer in a city celebrated for its legal aristocracy. Yet he soon became bored with the conventionality of the law. "My offices," he recalled later, "were always full. On one side of the waiting room the politicians gathered. Across the other side were my clients. After a few months I decided to choose between them and I chose the least stupid and the more honest." He chose the politicians.

Penrose wrote two short treatises during his early twenties, with enough stuff in them to establish him as an

American political historian of considerable rank. They reflect, again, the consistency of his political ideas. His history of the city government of Philadelphia remains to this day the most brilliant and concise summary of the topic. He wrote it together with his then law partner Edward P. Allinson; but it carries overbearing marks of Penrose's own style:

"We shall, in these pages, avoid the puerile error of complaining of the wickedness and corruption of professional politicians. It is very common to speak of that class as something outside of and apart from the ordinary citizen. . . . The politician, professional or otherwise, follows the stamp of his age; he is just what his age or environment demands or permits, neither better nor worse. The rules of his morality may differ from those of the clergyman or the merchant, but it weighs about as many ounces to the pound, and we are inclined to think that, from his intimate acquaintance with human nature, he gives better weight."

Penrose and Allinson published another masterful exposition, *Ground Rents in Philadelphia*, which examined the opportunities in Philadelphia for all kinds of people to own their homes. The number of citizens living in their own, separate houses was greater in Philadelphia than in any other great city in the world. Boies Penrose, who began his political career as Karl Marx died, recognized early one of the basic failures of the Marxist assumption: the failure to see that the so-called working classes, instead of being the most revolutionary and radical, were in reality the most conservative and property-minded elements of industrialized society, of the mass democratic state.

This was the last of Penrose's literary efforts. In the family history he wrote for the Harvard Class Record in 1881, he had called the early Penrose family "commercial rather than literary." The career he had chosen was neither commercial nor literary. Other people in politics, including certain proper Bostonians, could combine politics with literature. Penrose would not.

Two years after that frozen January day in 1885 when Penrose had taken the train to Harrisburg, he was elected state senator. Four years later, at the age of twenty-nine, he presided over the Pennsylvania Senate. Six years after that, in 1897, he was elected to the United States Senate, where he remained, growing ever more powerful, for twenty-four years; his was a political career that was spectacular at its outset, and solid for its duration, an impressive combination.

There was a curious duality about this career. In one sense it was not very different from that of the other political bosses of his period. While he governed the legislative process in a magisterial manner, his name was not connected with much important legislation. He reigned over his party in the Senate with the sleepy eyes of a grand vizier who had seen everything. Yet when legislation came before him, he spent hours examining it, making sure that it contained not even the smallest of legal loopholes. He shared none of that obsession with money that was typical of other bosses, and not only because he had inherited enough of it to keep him comfortable. Penrose presided over large secret financial transactions, involving the party machine, but none of his enemies could ever accuse him of having taken money for himself. This impressed the politicians around him. They cared for money. Penrose cared for power. This alone ensured their cooperation. When he found that politicians of his party, frenzied for loot, had gone overboard and were thrashing in deep water, Penrose said: "They're damned fools, not criminals." Yet he, who did not suffer fools gladly, went to considerable lengths to get them out of trouble.

In the manipulation of votes, Penrose was less cavalier and less scrupulous; yet even here his enemies could not pin him down with evidences of fraud. Penrose proceeded from the assumption that proper and assiduous management would ensure that American voters would select that which was accustomed and patriotic. One day he was watching a military parade march along Broad Street in Philadelphia. A companion, carried away with enthusiasm, said something about the admirable nature of this spectacle. The spectacle, Penrose said, that excited *his* unbounded admiration and deepest emotion "is a well-drilled body of voters marching in perfect and obedient order to the polls." Yet he was more than a master of getting out the vote. He also understood the importance of manipulating public opinion. In 1895 he and his ally, Pennsylvania Republican boss Matthew Stanley Quay, controlled much of the news reporting in the state through owning stock in a number of

Penrose at thirteen

newspapers. Penrose consorted with reporters, played host to them, dropped them all kinds of hints. In this respect he was a twentieth-century politician, rather than a surviving nineteenth-century one.

On the day of his first electoral triumph—and for some time afterward—the proper people were impressed. He was not impressed with them. He had concluded his treatise on Philadelphia ground rents with a scathing summary of the failure of the reform movement in Philadelphia. He read the manuscript before the Historical Society of Pennsylvania: it is not difficult to imagine the frozen faces of that distinguished audience, many of whom were members of the reform movement that this young lion in a den of Daniels dismissed in so many words. He had supported the reform charter for Philadelphia; but he was very skeptical of its results. The first mayor elected under the charter was a devout manufacturer, a bearded ropemaker named Edwin H. Fitler, who, Penrose said, was certain of the church vote "because he looks like a prosperous Apostle." Reformers were "watery-eyed," "pious fools." Their substance was thin. Many of his political allies feared the reformers; Penrose had only contempt for them. They were hypocrites. They prided themselves on having opinions more exalted than those of the common man, which made them feel good. Even more than the corrupt politicians, they depended on the support of the wealthier classes. "To whom did the reformers go when they needed the money to finance their campaigns of blather?" Penrose asked. "To the wage earners? Not by a damn sight. They went to the capitalists, to great merchants and manufacturers who, as it happened, themselves yearned to be legislators and write laws."

"There is more simplicity," Chesterton wrote, "in a man who eats oysters on impulse than in a man who eats Grape-nuts on principle." Penrose, who was a gargantuan devourer of oysters, the bigger the better, would have agreed. Yet his character was not simple. He had no scruples at all in presiding over the briberies spun out by his associates; he approved complicated plots whereby the latter would shortchange and defraud people through legislative legerdemain. His experience at law made him understand that even more important than the

letter of the law was the procedure in the courts: he had his minions fix juries, occasionally studding them with reliable veniremen with prison records. He succeeded in halting the proceedings against one of his men who had committed vote fraud. Yet no one could ever prove that any one of his own election victories depended on fraud. He cultivated his contacts with courthouse politicians, rumpled men with owlish faces who carried pints of whisky in brown paper bags. Yet he kept an impeccable staff of secretaries, and turned over his entire senatorial salary to the chief one among them.

His mail was voluminous; he made sure that every letter addressed to him received a prompt answer; he declined to use the congressional franking privilege on his personal mail. He had, as we have seen, an excellent prose style; yet his speeches are not interesting to read, and his letters are no more so. He wrote nothing that could cause him any kind of embarrassment. He was supposed to have boasted that he never wrote a letter to a woman "that you couldn't chill beer on."

He was a superpatriot; yet when his bitter political opponent Progressive Robert La Follette was about to be expelled from the Senate because of his opposition to the war against Germany, Penrose said that he would have no part of it, and later pulled strings to quash the expulsion motion. Both before and after World War I, Penrose was an unreconstructed isolationist; yet during the war he simply and squarely proposed that there ought to be "a dreadnought for every state of the Union." His mother had taken him to Europe during a Harvard vacation; after three weeks he asked to be allowed to return home. He was contemptuous of any kind of American involvement in the Old World; yet he was well versed in the classics. He was a collector of the first editions of travel books, of certain manuscripts, an amateur scholar of the history of explorations, and a voracious reader.

He was a genius at getting things done without working very hard. He knew how to delegate authority; his secretaries were tirelessly efficient. He was one of the first politicians to recognize the usefulness of the telephone as an instrument of instant, and unrecorded, contact; his bills ran to a thousand dollars or more a month. In 1914 his secretary persuaded him to purchase the large red Winton touring car

which became his trademark. He found it to be a useful vehicle for visiting all the counties of the state.

He sought the companionship of all kinds of people; yet he was essentially lonely. To his niece and nephew he was the classic uncle: a generous giant who spoke few words and was, perhaps, therefore especially impressive. He refused the invitations of Philadelphia dowagers with a bland formality. On the few occasions when he did appear at a dinner party, he was usually taciturn and bored, a graceless hulk of a man. He was surely different from other patricians of his era who had ventured into politics. It is difficult to imagine Boies Penrose contemplating the French châteaux as wiry, wispy Henry Cabot Lodge did, in the company of an intellectual wife with the tea-cake name of Nannie.

He never married; he never had a durable relationship with a woman. He was attractive to women when he was young; even when he had grown enormous, some of his attraction remained. He frequented brothels; these were especially numerous in the south end of the eighth ward, where he started his political career. His legendary appetites were reputed to have been sexual as well as alimentary. Yet during his career there was but a single instance when his enemies could pin the scarlet letter of scandal on his coattails. In 1895 he wanted to run for mayor of Philadelphia. At the last moment his nomination was withdrawn. The story was that the opposition had produced a photograph of Penrose issuing from a known house of prostitution. It was a grave disappointment, perhaps the greatest of his career.

In a largely unknown novel, *The Great One* by Henry Hart, the young protagonist—Penrose, only thinly disguised—has a searing and exceptional affair at Harvard with a beautiful society girl who flings herself at him on the rebound from an unhappy affair. Their affair, too, is unhappy and deeply wounds the protagonist. His carapace of cynicism hardens. The hero will never marry. This kind of construction seems plausible. (Hart knew Penrose well and at one time considered writing his biography.) Yet there is not a shred of evidence, or of family reminiscence, sustaining it. Penrose's sentiments about women remain a mystery.

His personal habits, too, were full of paradox. Penrose's strength and size made him a coveted candidate for the college football team. But he refused because he hated any kind of physical contact with other male bodies, especially muddy and sweaty ones. He hated to be touched. People who placed their hands on his arm or shoulder were pushed away; so was anyone who tried to lean close and whisper in his ear. He had a phobia of germs; yet his huge and hairless hands were often dirty, his fingernails unkempt. He had a fine dark head of hair; yet he, who made few compromises in his quest for comfort (he would leave his vest unbuttoned even on certain ceremonial occasions), wore large hats even on the hottest of days. He had an extensive wardrobe, with suits made of the best English cloth; they were often spotted with food stains. His boots were always polished, yet at times tied with string and, on one occasion, it was said, with a corset-string borrowed from a prostitute. He drank cheap gin and whisky in low dives. Did he have what the French call the *nostalgie de la boue*, the desire to wallow in the mud? Perhaps—but there is little evidence that he behaved indiscreetly. He kept his dignity at the lowest of tables and, perhaps, in the lowest of beds.

He was magnificently coarse. His eating habits were said to be gargantuan: a dozen eggs for breakfast, with twelve rolls, a quart of coffee, a half-inch-thick slab of ham; an entire stuffed turkey for lunch. There is the story told by Pennsylvania congressman J. Washington Logue, in whose presence Penrose had ordered reedbirds for dinner; the waiters brought a chafing dish containing twenty-six, which he proceeded to devour one by one, finishing the wild rice and drinking the gravy out of a cup, all of this after having drunk nine cocktails and five highballs. Yet Penrose cared little for luxuries: his favorite drink was Pennsylvania Highspire whisky. His table manners were ugly. Toward the end of his life he told the manager of the Bellevue-Stratford Hotel in Philadelphia to put a screen around the table when he was eating his lunch. Otherwise, he did not care. His sloth, too, was legendary. It grew with the years, eventually to be incarnated in the huge layers of fat which rendered him nearly immobile. Immobile, but not helpless. He was bearlike, not elephantine. In his youth, while hunting in Wyoming with his brother, the latter was badly mauled by a bear; disregarding the advice of the guides, Boies carried him out of the wilderness on his shoulders.

Penrose as a senior at Harvard
HARVARD UNIVERSITY ARCHIVES

Now he was the big boss of Pennsylvania, of the Republican party, in the Senate of the United States; friends and enemies alike called him Big Grizzly.

He hardly exercised in his later years; yet his strength did not desert him until near the end. It would be, I think, a mistake to speculate that his growing immobility, his sloth, was the result of hormonal imbalance, of a faulty metabolism. It was rooted, rather, in a deep and permanent sense of futility. There lay the tragedy of Penrose. He had an enormous appetite. He had little appetite for life.

He was born, he lived, he died in the same house. The furnishings were somber. He slept late, never engaged a cook, relied on a minimum of maid service. Penrose had no interest in traveling, even within the United States. His protectionist and isolationist preferences in politics were also the preferences of his private life. In 1915 he let himself be persuaded to buy a yacht, a broad-beamed, comfortable boat rebuilt to accommodate his dimensions. Around the *Betty* all kinds of legends sprang up, including one which had her anchored in the swells with a nude Penrose aboard, surrounded by politicians and floozies. According to others, Penrose never entertained a woman on his boat. The second version seems as believable as the first.

Were there two Penroses, a public and a private one: the tight-fisted, taciturn senator during the day, and the drunken orgiast at night? No, he was too much of a piece. His impassive face eventually congealed into a mask: but unlike other public personages in this century, it was his face that became the mask, not the public mask that became his face.

Penrose was a national figure for a quarter of a century. He entered politics at a moment when the generational guard was changing. McClellan, Grant, Arthur, Hancock, Seymour, Tilden—the Presidents and the presidential candidates of the period following the Civil War—all died within a year of Penrose's arrival in Harrisburg. He was a contemporary of Theodore Roosevelt and of Woodrow Wilson. He did not like either of them. The first was "a cock-eyed little runt," the second "a schoolmarm." He had no liking for Progressives of whatever stripe. He preferred the older type of boss, such as his ally Matthew Quay. He and Quay had considerable respect for one another, even though Quay was

compulsive about money. ("A plum" and "to shake the plum tree" were politico-financial metaphors that he brought into the American language. Penrose is reputed to have said that Quay "made it his policy always to keep at least one hand on the public purse. Only once in twenty years was there a state treasurer [Quay] could not control while he was in power. That state treasurer was Matthew Stanley Quay.") It is ironic that Penrose and Quay together played a decisive role in furthering the career of Theodore Roosevelt. They were behind Roosevelt's nomination to the vice presidency on the ticket headed by William McKinley in order to spite Quay's opponent Mark Hanna, the puissant boss from Ohio.

Penrose's association with corrupt politicians did little harm to his popularity. The secret (then called "Australian") ballot was enacted by reformers in Pennsylvania in 1891, with the intention of abolishing voting fraud. Penrose never had much trouble getting elected. The Pennsylvania legislature elected him to the United States Senate in 1896. Before the nomination Quay and his friends persuaded him to take on the front-running candidate, the merchant prince John Wanamaker, in a primary contest for popularity in Huntingdon County: Penrose won by nearly two to one. In 1913 the Progressives pushed through the constitutional amendment for the direct election of senators. It did not bother Penrose. In 1914 he beat his vocal opponent, the Progressive Gifford Pinchot, two to one again. His popularity was such that in 1915 the Republican organization considered carving a new county out of Luzerne and Schuylkill counties, to be called Penrose County. Penrose was not much interested, and the matter was dropped. In the taverns of the Philadelphia tenderloin district, autographed photographs of Penrose hung side by side with those of John L. Sullivan. The fact that Penrose considered it politic to support the city machine, even when it was proven to be awarding contracts to high bidders and charging the taxpayers double, hurt Penrose not at all. So much for the argument that people, expecially in the age of materialism, vote according to their pocketbook.

Penrose believed in the practicality of the capitalist credo. He supported large industries; he believed they made the United States great, since they provided ample work and high wages for the masses. He knew that industrial health depended on governmental rules

and regulations, foremost among them the high tariff walls that protected American industry from foreign competition. Like most Republicans, he did not believe in free trade or free competition; he thought the government ought to intervene on behalf of the industrialists. He advised steel magnate Henry Clay Frick not to fight the strikers. "Give 'em a little extra gravy till they settle down, then raise prices or the tariff to pay for it"—an inflationary philosophy of which Richard Nixon would have approved. At times Penrose could sound downright demagogic, thundering, for example, against the insidious invasion of margarine: "We are not willing that the profits of our domestic animals shall be taken away from their legitimate sources and given to a select syndicate of capitalists, in order that they may become inordinately rich." For "the profits of domestic animals" read the Pennsylvania dairy industry, as powerful in 1910 as it is today.

In 1914 the president of a Pennsylvania manufacturers' association declared that the divine purpose of the United States was, simply and squarely, to maintain "the best market on earth." Penrose did not really think of the United States in these terms; but he accepted, and welcomed, this kind of capitalist support as well as the support that had come to his party from the slush funds of small capitalists, even from the assessment of saloon keepers and brewers. His voting record was not moved by any consistent principle. He opposed four constitutional amendments: the income tax, the direct election of senators, woman suffrage, and prohibition; but he often changed his votes, backing away from causes when he sensed they had become unpopular. At times he would even propose and support reformist legislation. On occasion he actually led the fight against corruption. The Philadelphia Public Buildings Commission was a source of public robbery on a vast scale; and when, after long years, it was finally abolished, Penrose wired his crony in Philadelphia, State Senator James P. "Strawberry Jim" McNichol: "Splendid But What Steps Taken To Compel Commission To Take City Hall With Them?" He hated Philadelphia City Hall. There is an irony in this. That white-marbled, French-Victorian pile has become increasingly appreciated since Penrose's day as a national monument to the municipal mansard

*Penrose at the apogee of his power—
and bulk—photographed about 1915*
CULVER PICTURES

era, while Penrose Bridge and Penrose Avenue in South Philadelphia have remained the most depressing of thoroughfares, lined by dumps and the metallic filth of junkyards.

He did not hate reform, but he hated reformers. He would have agreed with Ambrose Bierce that a conservative is a statesman who is enamored of existing evils, as distinguised from a liberal who wishes to replace them with new ones. Was he a conservative? It is at least arguable that his opponent, the Progressive Pinchot, an early conservationist and a stern upholder of civic virtues, including prohibition, was a truer conservative. Penrose abhorred what he saw as the dry, the thin, the abstract virtues Pinchot represented. "Somebody told me that the man never had a drink in his life. If that's the fact, there's no use arguing with him. The man needs a drink." "You are a liability," Pinchot once wrote Penrose, "the most perfect living representative of the worst kind of politics in America." Penrose did not deign to answer but said that "Pinchot is as important as any cheap side show outside the fence of a county fair. He's as important as the tattooed man or the cigarette fiend." Penrose would have agreed with Burke's principle that politics must be adjusted not to reason but to human nature, of which reason is an important part but only a part. But Penrose was too much of a cynic to believe in principles; and in the age of democracy and of universal education, Boies Penrose had a lower estimate of human nature than had Edmund Burke of the untutored people of the eighteenth century. Burke said that the people must never be regarded as incurable. "The people are all right," Penrose said, "but their tastes are simple: they dearly love hokum." Penrose dearly believed in the efficacy of hokum. In 1919 a Washington newspaperman asked Penrose who would be the ideal Republican candidate for President. "We shall select a man of lofty ideals," Penrose said. "He shall be a man familiar with world problems. . . . He will be a man who will appeal warmly to the young voter—the young men and women of our country. A man of spotless character, of course. . . . A man whose life shall be an inspiration to all of us, to whom we may look as our national hero. . . . The man I have in mind is the late Buffalo Bill."

Penrose was a nationalist. He had a contempt for the foreign-born; he pushed through several acts to forbid or curtail their employment on public projects. He spoke out against the Yellow Peril, and introduced a Senate resolution in 1913 to send American troops into Mexico. In one of his rare foreign policy speeches, in 1914, Penrose said that the Mexicans were a bunch of shiftless Indians. At least the Spaniards had "compelled the Indian to work instead of lying comfortably. on the ground and letting ripe bananas drop into his mouth." He distrusted Europeans, and wanted to keep the country out of World War I. Yet by 1917 he realized that Americans were itching for war, and he chose not to swim against the current. After the war, he approved of the national revulsion against internationalism: "As far as I can ascertain, the League of Nations occupies an obscure place in the political cemetery of dead issues," he said. Disarmament was "a purely idealistic and nebulous theory." He may have been right, but for the wrong reasons. He had no interest in Europe, and disapproved of those who had, or pretended they had. When the Harding administration came in, one of Penrose's old Pennsylvania allies, Cyrus E. Woods, yearned to become ambassador to Spain. Penrose supported his nomination. Woods wrote an effusive thank-you letter, to which Penrose replied: "Dear Woods, I have your letter of June 15th, and am glad to hear from you. I congratulate you upon your appointment, although I frequently doubted the wisdom of your going abroad. I shall hope to see you before you leave. Yours sincerely, etc."

Talcott Williams, a Philadelphia journalist, recalled that in November, 1919, he had sat with Penrose in the latter's Senate committee room. " 'Senator,' " Williams asked, " 'what is going to be the great keynote of the Republican party in the next presidential election. The tariff?' [Penrose] said, 'No. I wish it was the tariff, but the tariff is beginning to seem like a back number.' There was a truthful utterance that I never expected to hear from Pennsylvania. I said, 'Well, I suppose you will take off the surtaxes on those big incomes.' 'No,' he said, 'I have sympathy with wealthy men.' I said, 'Penrose, you ought to have sympathy with wealthy men. You have touched them often enough.' [Laughter.] And smiling blandly upon me, he said, 'Talcott, don't be ribald. You are not writing an editorial.' I said, 'Well, what is going to be

the keynote?' He replied, looking the Roman senator, as he turned to me with those wide open eyes which all of us are familiar with when an idea had taken hold of him and he was going to drive it home. He said, 'Americanism.' I said, 'Senator, you are the man I have been looking for. What is Americanism?' He sank back into his chair in his committee room and he said, 'Dam'f I know, but I tell you Talcott, it is going to be a damn good word with which to carry an election.' "

So it was. Warren G. Harding, representing Americanism and normalcy, was Penrose's find. Penrose immediately saw that, in the age of photogravure, Harding's good looks, together with his conformism and his public relations experience would make him an excellent candidate. One day in early 1919 Penrose asked Harding to come over to his suite in the Willard Hotel. He addressed him point-blank: "Harding, how would you like to be President?" Harding liked the idea. Penrose and his ally Joseph P. Grundy, the chief of the powerful Pennsylvania Manufacturers Association, then began pushing Harding forward. Grundy presented Harding at an important dinner of the PMA. Harding made a speech emphasizing his homey Ohio background, including his membership in the local brass band. Penrose was too sick to attend. His secretary came back to Spruce Street to report on the speech. "He should have talked more about the tariff and not so much about playing the cymbals in the Marion Brass Band," Penrose said. The legend, according to which Penrose engineered Harding's nomination, is untrue. Grundy was the field marshal in Chicago; Penrose's doctors had forbidden him to travel, but he kept in touch by telephone (his bill for the convention month of July, 1920, was seven thousand dollars). Between Harding's nomination and the election, Penrose had but one piece of advice to the party: "Keep Warren at home"— the kind of sage advice which, had Penrose lived to the age of Methuselah, he undoubtedly would have offered to Gerald Ford.

By the age of fifty Big Grizzly had become a monster of a man. His enormous body was dominated by a mountain of a belly. His lips bit down in a face that was frozen dark with severity and contempt. He had come to resemble Field Marshal Ludendorff in mufti. He was at the peak of his political power; but he was as lonely as ever, saturnine and sardonic. "Boies," Quay once was supposed to have told him, "the people of Pennsylvania are going to demand more of you." "More what?" demanded Penrose. Perhaps his cynicism was not merely the result of political experience. To stand for being an aristocrat in a democratic world was so futile as to be ridiculous; but then, in the world of democratic politics, there was the futility of limited aspirations. He was choked with boredom. And now the mysterious symbiosis of mind and body asserted itself. He grew progressively ill with cancer, though it took a long time for this fact to be known. In 1919 he collapsed. His convalescence took a long time. On March 4, 1921, Harding came to the capital for his inauguration. By that time Penrose had to be moved around in a wheelchair. Woodrow Wilson, half-paralyzed, arrived at the reviewing stand. Penrose's secretary went up to the Secret Servicemen, offering Penrose's wheelchair to the stricken ex-President. Wilson, whose hatreds burned even more fiercely in sickness than in health, refused it.

And now Penrose's face had changed. It showed the ravages of the fatal disease. He had lost half his weight. His face had become impressive, almost beautiful again; his eyes were no longer beady but big and luminous. He became almost childish in his desire for approbation; there appeared in his conversation traces of kindness, even sentimentality. His Negro valet William Underwood, "Old Bill," was a lay preacher. One day he pushed Penrose's wheelchair toward the sun. "See here, William," said Penrose. "See here. I don't want any of your damned lies. How do I look? Am I getting any better? The truth now." "Senator," said William, crying, "I tell the truth. You ain't got long. Amen." "All right, William. Pray for me too." He died at sixty-one on the last day of 1921 in the Wardman Park Hotel in Washington, as he was waiting for the visit of his doctor. He was sitting on the edge of his bed, tried to stand up, fell back dead.

All his life Boies Penrose had an aversion to funerals. He had given orders for a spartan interment. There were to be no guests, no attendants, not even a clergyman. There was something terrible and solitary about this scene. The gates were kept closed by the police. Five high-wheeled black automobiles, containing fewer than ten people, including Penrose's three surviving brothers, drove to Laurel Hill, that most Victorian of cemeteries, filled during the nineteenth century with the grayed and yellowed and half-sunk mausoleums of rich ironmasters, deserted and empty. The grave was swept and garnished, the clods of earth were wet and dark. It was a day of cold black rain.

During the middle span of Penrose's life, Lincoln Steffens wrote a famous book on American cities, calling Philadelphia "corrupt and contented," a pair of adjectives that applied to Philadelphia politics at large; many people thought they also applied to Boies Penrose in particular. The truth was more complicated than that. Penrose had giant faults, but he was not personally corrupt. He had a giant appetite, but he was not contented. Beneath that mountainous flesh and behind that sternest of stoic countenances there lay, I think, the desperately solitary sadness of an unbelieving heart.

Penrose had left his estate to his three brothers. It amounted to a fraction of what his father had left him. The furnishings of 1331 Spruce Street were appraised at less than seventeen hundred dollars. His brothers found thirteen unworn suits, a dozen overcoats, four dozen new nightgowns, and in the cellar a stock of liquors appraised at a quarter of a million dollars. This last was legally theirs, since their brother had bought it before Prohibition became the law of the land, but a silly Pennsylvania law held that it could not be removed from the premises without a special permit of the state Prohibition director. Boies's brother, Dr. R. A. F. Penrose, a distinguished geologist, moved into the house. He made an abortive attempt at writing his brother's biography and died nine years later, also wifeless and childless. In 1934 the house was demolished to make way for a parking lot. A junk dealer paid four dollars for Boies Penrose's giant tub.

A sadly depleted Penrose, photographed in his wheelchair during his last years
CULVER PICTURES

☆ *John Lukacs is the author of many books. His most recent is* 1945: Year Zero, *published by Doubleday in 1978. This article has been adapted from a book in progress about certain Philadelphians.*

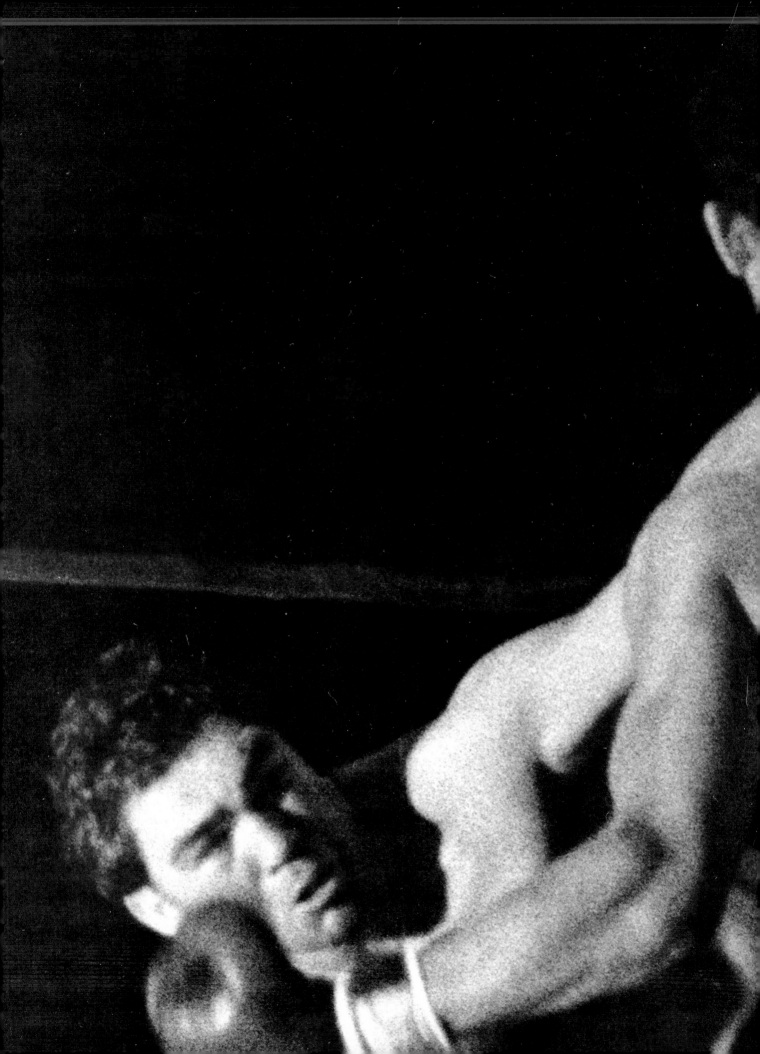

AMERICA'S GREAT BLACK HOPE

*When Joe Louis of the United States
met Max Schmeling of Germany
for the Heavyweight Championship
of the World in 1938, politics
and ballyhoo turned it into a
battle between Freedom and
Fascism — a foreshadowing
of World War II*

by Mark D. Coburn

A friend of mine still laments the deprivation he suffered after the first fight between Joe Louis and former heavyweight champion Max Schmeling of Germany in 1936. "I attended a dreary boarding school back then," he recalls. "Its only claim to excellence was the cinnamon rolls served for Sunday breakfast. Well, we were all boxing fans there, and those of us with sense knew that Joe Louis was unbeatable. When the odds were announced eight to one in Joe's favor, there was as much betting in that dreadful institution as the scarcity of Schmeling backers would permit. Imagine my delight when I chanced upon a fool willing to venture his two weekly cinnamon rolls against my pledge of sixteen. We were all distraught when the German knocked Joe out; but for me—at an age when eight weeks without rolls was an eternity—the future was a boundless Sahara, and it is well that no means of painless suicide was readily at hand."

Schmeling's win was an upset indeed, and my friend was not the only one to lose his bread on the Brown Bomber. But there was to be another day, another fight—perhaps the most "political" fight in boxing history—a symbolic encounter midway between a professional sporting event and a minor international incident.

Joe Louis (born Joseph Louis Barrow in Alabama in 1914) began boxing professionally, out of Detroit, in July, 1934. By the following May his record was 22-0, and most of his wins had been knockouts. Joe Louis was ready for the big time.

Luckily for the young boxer, the big time was also ready for a Joe Louis. It was twenty years since the Havana afternoon when Jess Willard, the Great White Hope, had dethroned Jack Johnson, the first black heavyweight champion. Johnson, to put it mildly, had not been popular with most white fans. They had seen him as cocky, "uppity." His way of toying with opponents stuck in the national craw. So did the fact that he had married two white women, and that he smiled as he battered white men into helplessness. In the years between Johnson and Louis an unwritten boxing law had kept black fighters from getting a crack at the heavyweight title, and in some states there were, for a time, legal sanctions against interracial boxing matches. But by the midthirties some of the racial tensions of Johnson's era had eased. The popularity of several black champions and contenders in lower weight divisions helped to make Louis' bid for the heavyweight crown acceptable. Then too, Joe Louis was splendidly cast for his role. In the vulgar parlance of the time, he was a "good nigger"; he "knew his place." Both by nature and through careful nurturing at the hands of John Roxborough and Julian Black, his managers, Louis was everything Jack Johnson before him and Muhammad Ali after him refused to be. The young fighter was modest, taciturn, generally gracious to those he fought. "And for God's sake," Roxborough had commanded his charge, "after you beat a white opponent, don't *smile!*" If Joe occasionally would do something peculiar, such as refusing to be photographed eating watermelon, still the tone and terms of his refusal could be called uppity only by out-and-out bigots. A phrase which today reeks of sanctimonious white supremacy hovered about the fighter throughout his career: Joe Louis, decreed the sporting press, was "a credit to his race."

The generally sad state of heavyweight boxing was also propitious to the advent of an exciting young fighter—even a black one. The years between Gene Tunney's retirement in 1928 and Joe Louis' climb to the title in 1937 were dominated by mediocre heavyweights. The tournament to pick Tunney's successor ended in 1930, with Max Schmeling the winner on a disputed foul over Jack Sharkey. By 1935, in the quickest turnover in boxing history, four more men had won the title: Sharkey (in a rematch memorable only for the lament spoken by Joe Jacobs, Schmeling's manager, "We was robbed!"); Primo Carnera (the "Ambling Alp," a huge but bumbling Italian fighter); Max Baer (the "Clown Prince," a boxer almost as amusing as Muhammad Ali, but not, alas, otherwise comparable); and James J. Braddock (the "Cinderella Man"—so called because his drab performances had nearly pushed him into retirement two years before he struggled his way up to the crown). Boxing historians regard Max Schmeling as the best of the lot, but the compliment is not overpowering. A new fighter with the 24-carat championship aura of a Dempsey or a Tunney was what the game needed, the experts agreed, but if no White Hope was to be found, maybe this Brown Bomber from Detroit would do.

Louis' sixth-round knockout of Carnera, in Yankee Stadium on June 25, 1935, made him a top contender. It was his first New York bout and his first fight promoted by Mike Jacobs, who, mainly because of his tie to Louis, would control New York boxing in the coming decade. After he beat Carnera, no one could deny Louis' right to a title fight on racial grounds. He would get a crack at Braddock if his fists earned one.

They almost didn't. By June, 1936, Louis had won four more fights, all by knockouts, including a four-round victory over Max Baer. Max Schmeling, who was making a comeback, was to be Louis' third ex-champion victim, and the fight was popularly regarded as Joe's last test before a title battle with Braddock. Schmeling would be the most skilled boxer Louis had yet faced; he was seasoned, intelligent, and professional, and he commanded a respect the crowds had never given the lumbering Carnera or the slapstick Baer. Some writers and fans believed there might be more than publicity behind Schmeling's cryptic comment that he had "seen something" to take advantage of in Louis' style. Nonetheless, Schmeling's record was marred by some losses, while Louis now had twenty-seven straight wins behind him and, at twenty-two, was Schmeling's junior by nine years. The powerful, beautifully built young slugger from Detroit appeared unstoppable. If the ten-to-one odds on Louis obtainable here and there seemed silly to those in the know, eight-to-one looked about right.

The Nazis were not happy about the match. To them, the notion of a competition between an "Aryan" and a Negro was dubious in the first place, and the likelihood of a Louis win did not improve matters. Reich authorities forbade a proposed excursion of German fans who planned to come to New York for the fight, and substantially the same Nazi attitudes toward Negroes that would flare up a few months later during the Berlin Olympics were smoldering when Schmeling left for the United States. There was no official send-off, and the fighter departed under a cloud of Party disapproval.

When the men entered the ring in Yankee Stadium, the ex-champion got more applause than the young contender. Max had always drawn well in New York, and few blacks could afford tickets for a big fight in 1936. This night Schmeling seemed cool, calm, every inch the old pro as he glared from under his thick, black eyebrows at Louis. More than one writer would remark the next day on

In the spring of 1936, when the baleful portrait at left was taken, twenty-two-year-old Joe Louis seemed invincible—especially to himself. Former champion Max Schmeling seemed no serious threat. "I thought I could name the round that I would knock Schmeling out," Louis recalled in his autobiography. Such overconfidence—plus a newfound enthusiasm for golf and an unabated delight in the company of the women who crowded around his training camp—poorly prepared him for the fight. The result (above) was a twelfth-round knockout victory for Schmeling. Louis spent the next two years bent on revenge: "Every time I fought a sparring partner," he remembered, "I couldn't get Schmeling out of my mind. Every partner was Schmeling to me."

PAGES 82–83: COLLECTION OF SAM ANDRE; LEFT: UPI; ABOVE: BROWN BROTHERS

Schmeling was never a Nazi, but he was a loyal German and a national hero. He is shown at the top dutifully "heiling" after a Hamburg ring triumph in 1935: the cigar being waved in a halfhearted salute at far right belonged to Joe Jacobs, Schmeling's American Jewish manager, whose presence was always an embarrassment to Hitler and his cohorts. Nazi leaders grew enthusiastic about Schmeling only when he demonstrated Aryan supremacy by knocking out Louis. At center, the Führer chats with Schmeling and his suitably blonde wife, Czech film actress Anny Ondra, after the boxer's victorious return from America. Such scenes had their effect in the United States, and by the time of the Louis-Schmeling rematch in 1938, feelings were running high on both sides of the Atlantic. The fighters themselves tried to ignore the political furor and concentrate on the coming bout: at bottom left, an apparently unconcerned Schmeling and his manager arrive in New York, and at bottom right, champion and challenger wait stoically to be weighed in, dressed as boxers were before show business transformed the game.

CENTER: UPI; ALL OTHERS: WIDE WORLD

the German's uncanny facial resemblance to Jack Dempsey.

That night Schmeling fought with care and precision—a style very different from Dempsey's furious attack, but, this night, at least, just as damaging. For three cautious rounds, neither man hurt the other. The fourth round was the turning point. Louis connected sharply with the already famous left jab, only to have Schmeling cross above it with a smashing right to the head. Another right followed, and Joe Louis was on the canvas for the first time in his professional career. Schmeling had indeed "seen something": he had seen that Louis tended to drop his right hand when he threw the left jab, thereby leaving his head unprotected.

The young boxer rose at the count of three, but the real contest was over. Although Louis would later say that he remembered little after the fourth round, he doggedly fought on, demonstrating the conditioning that would carry him through so many later years and fights; but it was all Schmeling's show. Time and again the right fist crashed on target and Louis was unable to retaliate save through occasional foul punches that he was perhaps too groggy to prevent. Well ahead on the judge's scorecards, Schmeling seemed resigned to plod through the full fifteen rounds, piling up points over his bewildered opponent, whose quivering legs refused to buckle. Then in the twelfth round, calling on some reserve of strength (and, he later claimed, fearing injury from Louis' low blows), Schmeling bore in with renewed vigor, caught the younger man cleanly on the jaw with a final right-hand blow, and the fight was over. Louis was still on his back, rolling from side to side, when referee Arthur Donovan's count reached ten.

The next morning, as the smiling winner chatted with the press, the Hitler regime suddenly changed its stance. From Dr. Paul Joseph Goebbels, Minister of Propaganda and National Enlightenment, came a cable to Schmeling: "To your wonderful victory my best congratulations. I know you fought for Germany; that it's a German victory. We are proud of you. Heil Hitler. Regards." Hitler himself sent Schmeling a telegram bearing his "felicitations," and to the fighter's wife, Czech-born film actress Anny Ondra, he sent a weighty basket of flowers. The day after that, the German press began demanding a Braddock-Schmeling championship bout in Germany. With-

in a week the same papers were explaining that Schmeling's victory demonstrated the supremacy of the Aryan race and that he had been inspired to fight his best through conversations with Hitler, Goebbels, and other Party leaders. Schmeling shortly returned home to be greeted by a large reception—at the Frankfurt airport—complete with speeches and circling *Luftwaffe* planes. It was announced that he would vacation as Hitler's guest. When the fight films were shown in Austria—where the Nazis were then struggling for power—cheering demonstrators surrounded the theaters. They shouted "Heil Hitler! Heil Deutschland! Heil Schmeling!" as, magnified on screens in Vienna and Salzburg, the right fist again and again smashed the Negro's jaw.

A Braddock-Schmeling fight was slated for New York—on June 3, 1937. It never took place. The full details of Max Schmeling's shoddy treatment by the American boxing establishment during the next year are too complex to unravel here; but not even the outraged howls of Goebbels' writers exaggerated greatly. In spite of his clear victory over Louis, Schmeling was denied a shot at Braddock's championship title. Louis got it instead. Why? An untangling of the charges and countercharges, the publicity and pleas, the court decisions and appeals, suggests one answer: money. Braddock's manager and the fight's promoters ultimately feared that anti-Fascist boycotts would hurt the gate, while a Braddock-Louis fight would draw well. On Janury 9, 1937, the Non-Sectarian Anti-Nazi League to Champion Human Rights announced a boycott of the ticket sales and of the proposed fight itself. By January 30 a host of other organizations had joined the boycott and threatened to picket bouts on Schmeling's proposed exhibition tour of several Southern states, where his win over Louis had been especially well received. Anti-Fascist groups decried the tour as "a piece of Nazi propaganda" designed to stir racism.

On January 31 Joe Gould, Braddock's manager, called a press conference to announce his acceptance of a $500,000 offer for a Braddock-Louis fight to be held in June in Chicago's Comiskey Park. "I have taken a poll of boxing writers all over the country," said Gould, "and the consensus is that a Braddock-Schmeling fight would draw only $200,000. Braddock is not responsi-

ble for political conditions that have arisen and will affect the drawing power of a fight with Schmeling."

Schmeling repeatedly said that he was a fighter, not a politician. He had never been close to the Nazi leaders, and he had a Jewish manager of whom they were known to disapprove. Publicity-wary promoters refused to listen.

So it was that on June 22, 1937, a new world's heavyweight champion sat in his dressing room in Comiskey Park. Joe Louis had knocked out Jim Braddock in the eighth round. It had been ten minutes before the loser was able to walk out of the ring. Years later Braddock would tell British boxing writer Harry Carpenter that he had never fought better than he did against Joe Louis. "But this...Louis was young, strong, and good. Oh, he was *good.* And I did my best, but come the eighth round, I was finished. I just hadn't anything left. And so when he hit me with that right, I just lay there. I couldn't have got off that floor if they'd offered me a million dollars to stand up."

As the South Side of Chicago and the black districts of other American cities and towns exploded in celebration (one estimate puts the Harlem crowds at one hundred thousand), the new champ was quietly opening one of the great publicity campaigns in sports history. Said Joe Louis to the scribbling reporters, "My only regret is that I did not have Max Schmeling in the ring tonight instead of the man I knocked out." After each of his three title defenses that year—and at some point during most interviews of any sort—Louis would repeat some version of that line. His sincerity was evident. He did not regard himself as the true champion until he had defeated the only man who had ever beaten him.

Schmeling also kept himself in the news during the year that passed between Louis' ascension to the championship and their rematch. After a visit to the Pompton Lakes, New Jersey, camp where the champion was preparing for his bout with Tommy Farr, Schmeling told the interviewers, "I want Louis." Once again he claimed that he "saw something" and that he was now "more eager than ever to fight him." He added, "I can lick him again." He shrugged off questions about his age: "Max has always lived a good, clean life. I can fight good when I'm thirty-five."

On December 13 Schmeling was in New York for a fight with a strong but undazzling journeyman named Harry Thomas. Despite the mediocre opponent and the inevitable boycott by the Anti-Nazi League, Schmeling's popularity and the aura beginning to surround the anticipated title bout drew a crowd of eighteen thousand, the largest gathering to see an indoor fight in New York in two years. Wrote one reporter, "Seven times Thomas went down under that short, flashing, paralyzing right-hand punch to the jaw with which Schmeling hammered Louis into submission." Joe Louis—always Joe Louis. Rarely was he absent from any press commentary on Schmeling as 1938 came in and the German went home to chop down two more opponents. Everything for both men was pointing toward their second encounter. The date finally was set for June 22, 1938. At least five American cities bid for the bout, but again Mike Jacobs lured the show into New York and Yankee Stadium.

Week by week the darkening political situation of 1938 seemed to add to the fight's special quality as a symbol of international and interracial tensions. The war was two years closer now than when Louis and Schmeling first battled, and even sports writers' phrases like "the Teuton" or "Herr Max" rang more somberly than they had in the summer of 1936. Sports and politics grew harder to separate. American coverage of Schmeling's tune-up fights and other activities now routinely included the reactions of the Nazi papers and sports authorities, the political mood of the German fight crowds, and Schmeling's Hitler salutes after his victories. Even Joe Jacobs, Schmeling's American manager, joined in the Nazi salute after one fight in Germany. "You gotta do it there or else," Jacobs explained. "Anyway I had my fingers crossed. I'm 560 per cent Jewish." In trying to promote Jewish acceptance of the second Louis-Schmeling fight, Jacobs volunteered a bizarre analysis of the political situation in the Reich: "Most of the trouble with the Jews over there is caused by the Jews in this country. Why, everybody's happy over there. Everybody's spending money like it was water, and talk of war makes the Germans laugh. Why, they even have synagogues still open over there. I know because I went to one three times one day. No one said anything to me because I was Jewish. They treated me like a king. . . ."

Meanwhile, a commentator for The Nation typified the strident tone of those who opposed the rematch. I. Q. Gross called Schmeling "a Nazi commodity" and Hitler's "close friend," and passed along a baseless rumor that "Schmeling is scheduled to take a leading post in Hitler's Cabinet as director of physical education for German youth, presumably to make them fit for the next fascist aggression." (During the war Schmeling would attain the rank of sergeant in the paratroopers—his highest "post" in the German government.) Gross went on to say that "thousands of Nazis, many in Storm Troop uniforms, have been ordered to attend the fight by officials of the German-American Bund."

Rumors and then counterrumors abounded. A German boxing expert said Schmeling would have to win by a knockout because American officials would not give him a fair decision. On this side of the Atlantic a story spread that Schmeling would be imprisoned by Hitler if he lost the fight to a black.

Joe Louis was a hero to large sections of the American black population, and that did nothing to ease the tensions surrounding the fight. Black feelings about the champion ran deep. When Louis beat Braddock, black militant Malcolm X once recalled, "All the Negroes in Lansing, like Negroes everywhere, went wildly happy with the greatest celebration of race pride our generation had ever known. Every Negro boy old enough to walk wanted to be the next Brown Bomber." The extra racial twist provided by Nazi pro-Aryan propaganda was not lost on American Negroes. Historian John Hope Franklin writes that after Schmeling knocked out "the athletic idol of the Negro race" in 1936, the average Negro could not speak of Nazis "without a feeling of personal antagonism." The racism engulfing Louis' career in the 1930's, if less ferocious than that of Jack Johnson's day, remained vicious enough—even without the addition of Nazi propaganda. It was not always pleasant to be a "colored" celebrity in America. A look through contemporary press coverage of the champion can make a modern reader squirm. The champion's speech was debased to make him a minstrel darky. Asked how he felt about using a bed where Washington had slept, he was supposed to have said, "Mistah Washington sho' know how to pick beds." A newspaper cartoon carried the caption: "Use the word 'defeat,' Joseph." "Sho. I pops 'em on de chin and dey drags 'em out by de feet." The sports editor of the New York Times explained that Joe would use no planned tactics against Schmeling because he was too stupid to master a strategy and fought by "instinct." The Literary Digest said that "one characteristic of Negro fighters is their inability to worry." The Denver Post held forth on Louis' fervent cravings for fried chicken. And so it went.

If the media presented the champion as slightly subhuman, at least his skills commanded respect. But the racism in articles on Louis' black fans was unrelieved. Story after story perpetuated the stereotype of blacks as rowdy, irresponsible, grinning children who lived for occasions to parade, gamble, sing, and dance. The Literary Digest spoke of Joe's fans as "the Harlem-tailored, gold-toothed, dark-hued gentry" (while calling the champion "the kinky-haired, thick-lipped . . . none-too-intellectual . . . shuffling, ex-Alabama pickaninny"). If Schmeling won, said the magazine, "there won't be a dime left in all Harlem."

On May 3, 1938, a cheering German crowd saw Schmeling off on the S.S. Bremen. Six days later he docked in New York, and the sports pages bannered: "Schmeling Arrives Confident He'll Beat Louis and Be First to Regain Title."

May passed into June as the two boxers trained. Fight talk blended with war talk, and the New York papers were filled with correspondence on whether or not the bout should be stopped. Promoter Mike Jacobs informed President Roosevelt that 10 per cent of his net profit would go to the Refugee Aid Committee. A nice gesture, but hardly enough to stem the flow to editors of letters concerned about Schmeling's share of the take. One from a Benjamin Solomon, of Port Jervis, New York, printed in the May 28 New York Times, was typical: To buy a fight ticket, said Mr. Solomon, was equal to buying goods made in Germany. "I don't see how anyone with a sense of decency would willingly do anything that helps the continuance in power of this regime of mass lying, mass tyranny, mass torture and mass murder!"

Schmeling looked sharp in training, the sports writers said. He was running ten miles a day (to Louis' six) and banging his sparring partners around. Louis looked poor; rumors had it that his intimates were troubled by his performance. On June 5 Mike Jacobs

Louis hammers Schmeling on the ropes—"It was all over in two minutes and four seconds," Louis said forty years later. "It was a long time coming, but now I felt like the 'real' champion. . . . Somebody was counting punches and said I must have hit Schmeling with near fifty blows . . . looking something like a pneumatic drill—and I guess that's what I felt like. God damn it, I won."

UPI

announced that reserved seats were moving to the tune of ten thousand dollars a day.

Retired ex-champion Braddock visited Louis' camp and picked the Bomber to win by a seventh-round knockout. "Joe seems to be concentrating on infighting and body punishing. Those are the tactics that should whip a veteran like Schmeling," said Braddock. But then Gene Tunney had gone to watch the contender and pronounced him to have the "finest right in the world today."

On the twelfth a crowd of 3,794 jammed Louis' camp at Pompton Lakes and paid $1.10 each to watch him in action. Jack Blackburn, the champ's trainer, said the fight would go one or two rounds if Max would stand up and slug. He added that Joe was a much better fighter for having taken a licking.

On June 19 the *Hamburg* docked with a party of twenty-five German fans, and more were due soon on the *Europa*; but the rumors of a huge contingent of German or German-American storm troopers seemed to be false. Mike Jacobs denied that the boycott by the Non-Sectarian Anti-Nazi League had done much damage at ticket windows.

Louis continued to look bad in training. Sparring partners were bouncing rights off him. One raised a welt under his left eye. Steve Dudas, the last man to fight Schmeling, had no doubts: Schmeling possessed "a left hook that no one in this country has ever seen. . . . It will be easy for Max."

June 22, the day of the fight, was hot and humid in New York, with a chance of rain. Louis weighed in at 200 pounds, Schmeling at 193. The champion was favored at two-to-one, but all seventeen experts polled by a German boxing paper picked Schmeling. NBC had combined its Red and Blue Networks to carry the broadcast on 146 stations. There was to be short-wave coverage and delayed broadcasts in several European countries. The usual 3 A.M. curfew was suspended in Germany so that cafés and bars could carry the fight for their patrons. Schmeling's wife would hear it as a guest in Goebbels' home.

All New York Central trains from the Midwest arrived carrying extra coaches, and the Pennsylvania line had also braced for a heavy passenger load. There would be thirty-six extra IND subways that night on the run to Yankee Stadium. Fifty Mexicans arrived in a private bus. Celebrity specta-

tors would include six mayors and several governors. The police announced that three thousand men would be specially deployed, including one thousand in uniform at Yankee Stadium, and another thousand added to the regular Harlem night shift.

On the comic page, Jeff, who had taken a beating that week as Louis' sparring partner, managed to defeat his opponent in a preliminary bout and now shouted to Mutt that he was ready to whip Louis and Schmeling simultaneously. Restaurants advertised quick prefight dinners for the fans. At Longchamps the boxing buff would find that it was "19 Minutes to Ringside from the Finest of Dinner Thrills." Loew's informed the public that all its theaters would announce the fight results, and the Palace promised to show a movie of the contest the next day.

It turned out to be a short film—two minutes and four seconds. Wrote Harry Carpenter, "No one can ever say for certain, but it is probable that in all of two and a half centuries of prize-fighting, those 124 seconds which Louis spent on Schmeling were the most concentratedly destructive."

In truth, Louis' onslaught lasted closer to ninety seconds. For the first half-minute the two men merely fenced and feinted. Then came two decent left jabs by Louis, seemingly a taunt to the challenger—a dare to use the right as he had done in the first fight. And the right came. It landed a little high on Joe's head, but solidly. It was Schmeling's first good punch—and his last.

Louis retaliated with a series of hard left hooks. A right hand slammed against Schmeling's head. Schmeling reeled into the ropes, his right arm hanging over the top strand. Louis raced in with a series of body blows, mainly rights, one of which landed far back on the left rib cage. After the fight Schmeling would say he'd been fouled, but no formal claim was filed and he soon withdrew the accusation. The films show that the punch was clean by New York rules. It fractured Schmeling's third lumbar vertebra and likely drove it against his kidney. The shock half paralyzed Schmeling's legs. His scream of pain was audible many rows from ringside above the uproar of the seventy thousand shouting spectators.

Louis kept firing—swift, body-ripping blows, thrown from a slugger's flat-footed stance. Schmeling did his best to withstand the onslaught. Seeing the films today, one is awed not by the fight's brevity but by its length—how

could the German endure so much?

Seemingly frozen by Schmeling's shriek, referee Donovan took a few seconds before stepping in, waving Louis back, and beginning to count for a standing knockdown. Schmeling lurched off the ropes and wove toward the center of the ring. Louis met him, and a left and a furious right to the head sent the challenger to the canvas for a count of three. No veteran in control of himself would have risen so soon.

Louis attacked again. A left and a right snapped Schmeling's head around and dropped him for a second time. He landed on his knees, his hands lightly resting on the floor, and, incredibly, rose at the count of one. A fierce left hook and yet another of Louis' whistling rights sent him tumbling for the last time. As his back twitched convulsively on the canvas, his trainer threw in the towel. That gesture of surrender was no longer recognized in New York, and the referee whirled and threw the cloth out of the ring. When he turned back to Schmeling (the timekeeper's count stood at five), Donovan saw that the challenger was helpless and waved his arms to end the fight.

Schmeling was soon up, his face unmarked, and was able to push through the mob in the ring and congratulate the winner. Shortly thereafter he was rushed to a hospital, his driver taking a circuitous route to avoid the bedlam in Harlem. As Louis' fans filled the twenty blocks of Seventh Avenue closed off for street dancing, cables from Goebbels and other ranking Nazis began to arrive expressing condolences and assuring everyone that Max would not be arrested. As the columnists hurried to file stories abusing Schmeling for crying foul or instructing him on what to tell Hitler when he got back to Germany, ten thousand hometown fans danced in the streets of Detroit beneath a waving banner that proclaimed, "Joe Louis Knocked Out Hitler."

There was black jubilation in the rural South, too—of another, quieter kind. President Jimmy Carter told part of the story in his autobiography, *Why Not the Best?:* "All of our black neighbors came to see Daddy when the second Joe Louis–Max Schmeling fight was to take place. There was intense interest, and they asked if they could listen to the fight. We propped the radio up in the open window of our house, and we and our visitors sat and stood under a large mulberry tree nearby. . . . My father was deeply disappointed in the outcome. . . . There was no sound from anyone in the yard, except a polite 'Thank you, Mister Earl' offered to my father. Then, our several dozen visitors filed across the dirt road, across the railroad track, and quietly entered a house about a hundred yards away out in the field. At that point, pandemonium broke loose inside that house, as our black neighbors shouted and yelled in celebration of the Louis victory. But all the curious, accepted proprieties of a racially segregated society had been carefully observed."

Before morning a rumor that Max had died from the beating he took was spreading through New York. The *New York Times*'s switchboard handled twenty-one hundred calls about his condition, and the hospital's phones were so badly tied up that it was compelled to issue radio bulletins.

The next day the German press said that the fight was too short to prove much. One German fan was quoted as saying, "Yes, Schmeling may have been almost killed, but Beethoven's Ninth Symphony still lives on."

As a symbol of American strength in a time of growing world tensions, as an American rebuttal of Nazi racist propaganda, and as a sweet moment for black Americans in an era filled with bitter ones, the Brown Bomber's triumph over the Teuton became a memory to savor.

The fight still survives as memory and symbol, but even two weeks after the bout its intrinsic unimportance in world affairs was clear. As the ship carried Max Schmeling—still bedridden—back toward Europe, in early July, and as the champion's managers sought new opponents, there was no evidence that the march of events toward another world war had been hastened or hindered in the slightest by Joe Louis' fists.

Schmeling's arrival in Berlin, July 9, was less important sports news for Americans than yesterday's baseball scores. It was, to be sure, a tribute to Louis' power that Max still sometimes needed support when he walked, but the notion that the loss to a Negro might lead to a prison term for a gallant, aging sportsman who had done his best was too ridiculous to bring up again. The hullabaloo was over. Max Schmeling was home. The quiet crowd that greeted him numbered about two dozen.

☆ *Mark D. Coburn teaches English at Fort Lewis College, Durango, Colorado, and writes on American topics.*

Harlem gets the news.
UPI

LINCOLN BEACHEY

"They call me the Master Birdman," he said once, "but they pay to see me die." He hated his audience. He loved his audience. He was bitter, contradictory, expansive, and fatalistic. Foremost in the first generation of daredevil pilots, he flew in a natty pin-striped suit with a two-carat diamond stickpin keeping his necktie in place. His fellow pilot Beckwith Havens, one of his very few close friends, described him as "a strange, strange man." He was also, according to Orville Wright, who knew something about it, "the most wonderful flyer I ever saw and the greatest aviator of all." He claimed to have flown for twenty million people—and he flew wide enough and far enough for that to be possible.

Lincoln Beachey was born in San Francisco in 1887. While still in his teens, he made his way east to Toledo, where he got a job in the balloon factory of a man named Charles Strobel. He wanted to fly, but Strobel refused to let him, so Beachey started spending his nights in the factory, sneaking out at dawn to take up the airships. After a few weeks of ghosting around over the sleeping town, he told Strobel what he had been doing, and demanded an aviator's contract. He got it.

By 1905 he was the best in the business, and sometime in 1910 he decided to shift from airships to airplanes. It was a typically reckless Beachey decision; more than thirty pilots died that year trying to put their wood, wire, and canvas machines through paces beyond their capabilities. Impressed by his reputation as a balloonist, the Wright brothers offered to take him on as an exhibition flyer, but the money wasn't good enough, so he went to Hammondsport, New York, where a gifted inventor named Glenn Curtiss was building airplanes. Curtiss gave him a tryout, but Beachey immediately wrecked the plane. "His big trouble," his brother Hillery said, "was that he wanted to stick it right up into the air. There wasn't enough power to do it. . . . He broke up several of Curtiss' planes. . . . Curtiss was afraid to look—just turned away when he first saw him fly." But Curtiss' exhibition manager saw something in Beachey's flailings and browbeat Curtiss into sticking with the impetuous would-be pilot. It turned out to be the best publicity investment Curtiss ever made, for as soon as Beachey got the hang of handling an airplane, he flew like a drunken angel.

In an era when most people were awed just by the sight of a plane in the air, Beachey could make his primitive machine do almost anything. Bucking and twisting across a field, he would angle down to pick up a handkerchief off the ground with his wing tip. Then he would climb a mile up, cut his engine, and go into his "death dip," a vertical dive that had women in the crowd fainting.

Beachey's first summer's record is an indication of his ability. In June of 1911, with 150,000 people watching, he dove into the gorge of Niagara Falls, came out through the spume at the base, and flew under the International Bridge. With his carburetor sucking spray and his engine failing, he barely managed to scramble up from the boiling rapids to the safety of the Canadian shore. He never tried that particular stunt again, and neither has anybody else.

A month later he picked up a five-thousand-dollar prize for flying from New York to Philadelphia. Two weeks after that, he set the world's altitude record by topping his fuel tank and then simply climbing as fast as he could until, in the arctic air currents more than two miles up, his gas ran out.

If he celebrated after he glided back to earth, it wasn't with liquor. "One glass of champagne, and he'd be tight," Havens recalled, surprised by Beachey's abstemiousness in an age when at least one of his fellow pilots drank so hard his mechanics had to lift him into his plane. Beachey's failing, "a real strong weakness" according to Havens, was women; he left a string of disappointed "fiancées" behind him as he barnstormed around the country.

Suddenly, at the height of his fame in 1912, Beachey announced his retirement. "I have defied death at every opportunity for the last two years," he said. "I have been a bad influence, and the death of a number of young aviators in this country can be traced, I believe, to a desire to emulate . . . my foolishly daring exploits. . . . You couldn't get me in an airplane again at the point of a revolver."

This moody resolution was short-lived. Beachey had spent a few miserable months on the vaudeville stage when he got word that a Frenchman had looped the loop. "If he can do it, so can I!" Beachey shouted, and told Curtiss to build him a special stunt plane. Soon he was barnstorming again, charging five hundred dollars for his first loop and two hundred for each that followed. "That was . . . in the Middle West where William Jennings Bryan was talking," his brother remembered proudly. "I think they both got a thousand dollars a day, Bryan and Lincoln Beachey."

He had baited what he called the "scythe-wielder" more than most of his generation by the time he came to San Francisco for the Panama Pacific Exposition of 1915. "The old fellow and I are pals," he said, but he was obviously feeling strain, and occasionally behaving erratically. Once, when the governor of the state stepped forward to congratulate him after a flight, Beachey turned away, went back up, and, circling the field, stripped off his clothes. When he landed, he snarled to his mechanic, "Let's hear what he has to say about me now."

On March 14 he came out to his machine looking grave and troubled. His mechanics thought he had some sort of premonition of disaster, but fifty thousand people had come to see him, and he went up. He looped over the bay, then lowered the plane's nose for the death dip. Aviators among the spectators said he was dropping at nearly three hundred miles per hour when the wings tore away.

While the stunned crowd watched silently from the shore, a diver from the battleship *Oregon* located the plane, and thirty-five minutes later it was hoisted from the bay. They found Beachey tangled in the wreckage, his hands torn from his desperate struggle to free himself. America's greatest stunt pilot had drowned.

GENTLEMEN AFIELD

They went to the woods with rod and gun— and gloves, servants, caviar, and champagne

by John G. Mitchell

A strange word suddenly appeared in the American vernacular after the Civil War. The word was "sportsman." It served to define a certain kind of gentleman who took his leisure with rod and gun. And that was the curiosity of it, for the pursuit of fish and game on this continent had seldom before been associated with leisure. One hunted or fished in order to eat. The rod and the gun rested next to the ploughshare. Men who went afield for amusement were regarded as scalawags undoubtedly cursed with addiction to liquor, cards, and cockfights as well. But the war, and the onrushing force of the industrial revolution, had somehow rolled part of the Puritan ethic aside. Now, rod and gun could be perceived not only as tools of subsistence but as accouterments of a new aristocracy. Now, more often than not, the fellow with burrs on his cuffs would be hailed as a pillar of the community.

By most hindsight accounts, the last quarter of the nineteenth century and the first decade or two of the twentieth fall within a period that might fairly be called the gilded age of field sports. In the cities of the East, thousands of well-to-do gentlemen turned toward the out-of-doors with a passion and a purpose that would have shocked the sensibilities of their pragmatic forefathers. Bankers and lawyers, doctors and professors, merchants and ministers donned their heavy tweeds and streamed into the countryside in quest of woodcock and quail and mallard and deer and trout. From Baltimore they sallied forth to Chesapeake

Bay, from Pittsburgh and Philadelphia to the Poconos, from New York to the Catskills and the Adirondacks, from Boston to the wildwood of Maine. Some ventured even into the sylvan reaches of Canada, while in the South elaborate expeditions sought game birds of various kinds. And always the sportsmen went in the company of their peers, for the common workingman had neither the time nor the means to participate. To be properly afield in the gilded age, one necessarily had to be affluent, and preferably to the manner born.

There was a measure of incongruity about this new American sporting breed. It seemed to be influenced by something old, something new, something borrowed, something blue. Old was its admiration for the crisp, efficient style of British aristocrats who had been dropping grouse on the tamed Scottish moors, or dredging trout from the chalk streams of Devon, for more than a century. New was the Americans' fascination with wilderness; Britons had not experienced *that* on native ground for one thousand years. Borrowed was the Old World's proper code of sporting conduct, which would soon crimp the style of stateside poachers and market hunters. And blue was the blood of the gentry; or possibly, in later years, the melancholy understanding that one might well outlive the end of the game.

Inevitably, the growing popularity of the field sports inspired a number of specialized journals. The first with a continentwide circulation was *American Sportsman*, appearing in 1871. Two years later, *Forest and Stream* made its debut, followed by *Field and Stream* (1874) and *American Angler* (1881). Each more or less subscribed to the philosophy advanced by *American Sportsman* in an early issue. Sportsmanship, an editorial asserted, was not "in the killing of numbers," but rather in "the vigor, science, and manhood displayed—in the difficulties to be overcome . . . and lastly in the true spirit, the style, the dash, the handsome way of doing what is to be done,

On one of the Adirondacks' countless ponds, two nineteenth-century sportsmen set out for a day's fishing with justifiable confidence.
THE ADIRONDACK MUSEUM

and above all, in the unalterable love of fair play. . . ."

The most influential of these journals was *Forest and Stream*, a weekly devoted to "Field and Aquatic Sports, Practical Natural History, Fish Culture, The Protection of Game, Preservation of Forests, and the Inculcation in Men and Women of a Healthy Interest in Outdoor Recreation and Study." Charles Hallock of New York was its first editor, and he quickly defined the weekly's constituency. *Forest and Stream*, he promised, was not for "the fish hog, the night hunter, the pseudo-sportsman"; it would "pander to no depraved tastes, nor pervert the legitimate sports of land and water to those base uses which always tend to make them unpopular with the virtuous and good."

In addition to editing the journal, Hallock traveled extensively afield. In 1878 he shared his knowledge of the out-of-doors in a remarkable volume entitled *The Sportsman's Gazetteer and General Guide*. It soon became the sportsman's bible, for it was packed with detailed information on the natural history of fish and game species, the care and training of sporting dogs, the proper selection of rifles and shotguns, the uses of decoys and blinds, and the dressing of artificial trout flies. *The Gazetteer* also provided basic training in the art of "woodcraft."

Comfort in camp, Hallock advised, should be every hunter's "main business." In sleeping, "No more cover should be used than will keep the body at natural heat. . . . Keep your feet to the fire, but don't let them burn." Coffee grounds, said Hallock, are "very useful to keep fish fresh. . . . [Sprinkle] thickly into the belly and mouth . . . the more grounds used to each fish the better." In walking, he urged the sportsman always to run his eye along the trail "at least a rod in advance." And he favored the use of one's felt hat in drinking from forest pools, for if one sipped the water while lying flat on the stomach, there was "a real danger of swallowing living creatures that may possibly cause serious difficulty afterwards."

Hallock's bible also provided what may well have been the first comprehensive directory of "principal resorts for fish and game" in North America. Not surprisingly, it found little to recommend in the West. Of New Mexico, for example, Hallock reported that "The greater portions of the entire territory . . . are occupied by vast sterile plains [and] . . . are subject to the incursions of the Apaches. . . . for the sportsman, New Mexico has few attractions."

Hallock's Atlantic seaboard constituents, in any event, were not much attracted to *any* part of the West. A few, such as George Bird Grinnell, Hallock's successor as editor of *Forest and Stream*, did cross the Plains to the Rockies and beyond in quest of big game; and later, Theodore Roosevelt would write glowing reports of sporting under the big sky. But for the most part, the Eastern gentry looked to its own backyard. And with good reason. The Dakotas were infested with ruffians and louts, but only gentlemen went afield in the Adirondacks.

O f all the popular fish and game "resorts," the Adirondack region of New York surely reigned as number one during the last quarter of the nineteenth century. Though its woods were no wilder than northern Maine's, they possessed a singular physiographic advantage found nowhere else in the East (with the sole exception, on a smaller scale, of Maine's Rangeley Lakes district). The advantage was a vast network of interconnected lakes and streams navigable by pirogue and guideboat. One could travel for miles without soiling the collar or blistering the feet. The gentry then was not much enamored of tramping.

For the first generation of sportsmen, it might be said that the Adirondacks were discovered in 1869 by William Henry Harrison Murray, a Boston clergyman with strong faith in the recuperative power of balsam-scented air and a certain flair for fact mixed with fiction. In the spring of that year—on or about April Fool's Day, according to one chronicler—there appeared in the bookstalls of Boston and New York a thin volume by Murray entitled *Adventures in the Wilderness; or, Camp-Life in the Adirondacks*. By whatever standard best sellers were measured in those days, Murray's opus was soon among them. By June, the stampede was on as readers rushed from their city homes and offices to book passage to Murray's "Sportsmen's Paradise."

There was much sensible information in Murray's book. He emphasized simplicity of dress: stout pantaloons, a felt hat, and buckskin gloves were *de rigueur*, and for the ladies, a "net of fine Swiss mull . . . to slip over the head . . . and you can laugh defiance at the mosquitoes. . . ." He listed as necessary provisions only coffee, tea, sugar, pepper, potatoes, pork, and condensed milk, for the staples would be venison and trout. He urged caution in the selection of

Although built in appropriately rustic style, many turn-of-the-century hunting and fishing "camps" were lavishly appointed.
BROWN BROTHERS

Above: Some gentlemen hunters were trophy addicts, as the décor of their hunting lodges attested. The owner of this collection in the Adirondacks evidently hunted abroad as well as locally. Left: Clubs and hotels provided comfort for ladies and children while the men went afield; this is the Ausable Club.
BOTH: THE ADIRONDACK MUSEUM

Above: With a dead animal for every hunter, this picture of a deerslayers' rendezvous around 1880 suggests why the North Woods of Maine were considered a sportsman's paradise. Right: When wives decided to go camping along with their husbands, the amenities of tent life had to be augmented.

ABOVE: CULVER PICTURES; RIGHT: ESSEX COUNTY HISTORICAL SOCIETY, ADIRONDACK CENTER MUSEUM

guides: "With an ignorant guide you will starve; with a lazy one you will lose your temper." He described the alternate routes of access; one was by rail to Lake Champlain, by steamer to Port Kent, by coach to Keeseville, whence, by whatever mode available, one traveled fifty miles over a plank road to Martin's Hotel on the Lower Saranac. And all manner of sporting, wrote Murray, was "easy and romantic." A mixture of sweet oil and tar would fend off biting insects. As for other troublesome critters, there were none to fear: "Now, fortunately, the panther is almost wholly unknown in this region."

Murray, however, was not content with guidebook prose. Fiction began to overtake fact. There were incredible waterfalls which Murray and his trusty guide had shot in their boat; there were "a thousand lakes, many yet unvisited"; there was a "Nameless Creek" where *pairs* of two-pound trout leapt to the cast of every fly. Readers who hastened to the mountains found no undiscovered lakes or nameless creeks; nor did they find the sporting that easy and romantic. But the disenchanted, dubbed "Murray's Fools" by a mocking press, in short time were replaced in the woods by a sizable cadre of sophisticated sportsmen who could wink at the author's tall tales and still be grateful for the rest of it. In fact, Murray had been far more accurate about the Adirondacks than most of the writers of his day. One J. T. Headley, for example, claimed in 1849 that Tahawus (Mt. Marcy) was the second highest mountain "in the Union"; it actually measures 5,344 feet.

As the sportsmen and their families became acclimated to Adirondack summers in such hostels as Martin's and Bartlett's on the Saranacs and Paul Smith's at St. Regis Lake, some began to think of settling into places of their very own. Soon there were private camps and clubs and preserves in the mountains, where the wealthy could be assured of compatible company, unencumbered by the likes of Murray's Fools.

There have been endless unresolved arguments over the years as to whether the first "camps" were established in the Adirondacks or the Maine woods. It matters little. In all likelihood the camp phenomenon developed simultaneously in both regions with the same results—the presence, deep in the woods but invariably with a view of blue water, of structures designed for roughing it with most of the comforts of home.

In Maine, wealthy sportsmen from Boston's Beacon Hill and Brookline staked their claims on the island of Penobscot Bay, at Mt. Desert, at Moosehead, Sebago, Kennebago, and the Rangeley Lakes. The inland camps tended to be more rustic than the ones along the coast, where ease of access by steamer encouraged the transformation of early modest camps into elegant estates. But none of the gentry referred to his place in such lofty terms. Be it ever so elegant, there was no place like "camp." And no other word for it, either.

The authentic Maine or Adirondack camp was the height of luxury transplanted to the wilderness. Generally there was a main lodge with four or five outbuildings. The windows and doors were trimmed in green paint. Meats and produce were kept fresh in the icehouse. For lunch the guest had a choice of squab or *filet mignon*. Often, lunch was taken far afield from the camp; a guide was required to carry provisions for every two family members or guests. Tablecloths were spread on the spruce needles. Wine was chilled in the brook. Some camp owners imported tutors and nannies for their children. While the men of the camp were off hunting or fishing, womenfolk sat in the shade by the shore. They played at cards and read the latest novels. They inhaled the salubrious air. They were grateful to be far from the malodorous city, where malaria and typhoid were taking their ghastly toll.

By the 1880's, some camp owners in the Adirondacks were incorporating as shareholders in private clubs. The clubs began to purchase large tracts of the forest as hunting and fishing preserves. In some areas, fences went up—and no-trespass signs. In 1892, the New York State Forest Commission estimated, a full quarter of the Adirondacks was held as preserve by clubs, associations, and individuals. Morgans, Whitneys, Vanderbilts, and Rockefellers presided over vast woodland retreats. Near Old Forge, the Adirondack League Club purchased a hundred thousand acres. To the east, the Ausable club held some thirty thousand acres along one flank of the High Peaks.

Old "Adirondack" Murray saw what was happening, and he didn't like it. Two years before his death in 1904, in an article for *Field and Stream*, he denounced the posting of large properties in his beloved mountains. "There are on the

Dr. J. R. Romeyn, a gentleman angler of the day, displays reserved enthusiasm on a trout stream near Bartlett's fishing camp in the Adirondacks.
THE ADIRONDACK MUSEUM

earth," he wrote, "certain creations too precious to man; too essential to his welfare to pass under private ownership." But the landowning gentry did not see it as Murray did. If they were to prolong the sport, in the face of increasing pressures on fish and game, the gentry reasoned that private ownership was the only way left for them to go.

By the turn of the century, another part of New York had attained a certain vogue among sportsmen, especially those whose bias ran in favor of trout and the art of angling for them with the artificial fly. The brooks of the Catskills were teeming with trout. There seemed to be something special about the chemistry of such streams as the Beaverkill, Willowemoc, and Neversink—a mineral in the water, perhaps; or possibly some entomological gift from the gods—that gave them surpassing excellence as habitat not only for the native brook trout, but for the transplanted Western rainbow and the wily, imported European brown as well.

About this time, a Pennsylvania angler named Theodore Gordon returned to America from a visit to England. There, from the banks of the old country's trout streams, he had watched English anglers manipulating a new kind of fly. Unlike the wet flies then in vogue in America, this one—properly dressed—floated on the surface of the water.

Gordon hastened home to anoint the dry fly in American waters at Junction Pool, where the Willowemoc joins the Beaverkill near Roscoe in Sullivan County. To a large extent, it was a baptism for the region as well as the fly. Without benefit of a best-selling book or even a mocking press, Gordon and his floating flies opened the Catskills to a rush of anglers as surely as Murray had piped them into the Adirondacks a generation before. Up the long grade from the Hudson they came in the parlor cars of the New York, Ontario & Western, to Frank Keener's Antrim Lodge and other inns catering to the fly-fishing trade; and later, as the pressure mounted in numbers of anglers and streamside space, to the private clubs and preserves at Balsam Lake and Debruce. Already the experience of the North Woods was repeating itself in the Catskills. But time at last was running short for the gentle sportsmen of the Eastern seaboard.

The breed itself was not without blame. It had preached a rigid code of conduct—that the hunter or angler should never take more than his table might need. But the sporting class was not unlike any other: there were always a few who would rub against the grain. One early visitor to the Adirondacks boasted in a hotel register that in only a few weeks time he had taken 350 brook trout, 39 partridge and woodcocks, and 2 deer. And just six years after publication of his controversial book, Preacher Murray was moved to lament that "stupid greed" had already diminished the trout and deer of the Adirondacks. He did not explain that a certain amount of pragmatic greed was needed then just to feed the camps and inns his book had inspired; or that in one summer month he had slaughtered five deer with his own rifle. Despite tighter game laws over the years, similar excesses continued into the twentieth century.

The gilded age of the field sports had begun at a time when the population of the United States stood at 30,000,000. By 1900 it had grown to 76,000,000; by 1920 to 106,000,000. By 1920, too, the old plank roads into the mountains had been paved with hardtop, and the wealthy (and even some of the not-so-wealthy) were out upon them in their Model T Fords. The length of the work week had dwindled. Factories and offices were beginning to buzz with the prospect of paid vacations. The number of licensed hunters had doubled in ten years, and mass-production techniques were turning out rifles and shotguns at half the prewar cost. On opening day of the trout season, anglers stood elbow to elbow at Junction Pool. Campers thought twice before drinking from forest pools; in time they'd have halazone tablets.

To be sure, the good life in the deep woods has not vanished altogether. Even today there are still a few elegant camps in Maine, clubs in the Poconos and Catskills, preserves in the Adirondacks where the wealthy may yet pursue the pleasures of forest and stream—when they are not otherwise engaged on the golf course, the tennis court, or the ski slope. New words and phrases are being bandied about on the summer porches of the lingering woodland retreats. The word "sportsman" is not often among them.

☆ *John G. Mitchell is a field editor for* Audubon Magazine *and a frequent contributor to our pages.*

AN ARTIST-SPORTSMAN'S PORTFOLIO

*A. B. Frost faithfully recorded
the woodland pursuits of himself
and his affluent friends*

Arthur Burdett Frost, who at the turn of the century was perhaps the best-known and most popular illustrator in America, sketched and painted his way from relatively humble beginnings to hobnobbing with the leisure class. A significant element in this ascension was his lifelong fascination with sports of field and stream: he often hunted and fished with gentlemen of affluence, and depicted their passionate pursuits on paper and canvas with such accuracy and verve that they came to consider him the sportsman-artist *par excellence.*

A. B. Frost (as he signed himself) was born in Philadelphia in 1851. He worked as an apprentice engraver and lithographer as a boy, and studied briefly with Thomas Eakins at the Philadelphia Academy of the Fine Arts. In his early twenties he was lucky enough to be chosen to illustrate a humorous book by Max Adeler, *Out of the Hurly Burly* (1874), which became an international best seller. The resulting publicity got him a job at the New York *Graphic*, where he drew political cartoons and may have invented the donkey as the symbol of the Democratic party (some credit Frost's artist friend Thomas Nast). Joining the staff of *Harper's Weekly* in 1878, he turned more to the illustration of various manly sports including, naturally, hunting and fishing. His range during his long and industrious career was wide, however, and with the general public his fame hung chiefly on his charming pictures for Joel Chandler Harris' *Uncle Remus and His Friends* (1892) and its enormously popular sequels. He also painted more formal illustrations for such magazines as *Scribner's* and *Collier's.*

Frost's hunting and fishing paintings, which are well exemplified here, combined close attention to details of equipment, costume, the terrain, and the quarry, with a peculiarly vivid sense of the immediate moment and the personalities of the sportsmen and even their dogs. Frost died in 1928, a lover of rod and gun all of his life.

*In 1895 Charles Scribner's Sons
brought out a large-format portfolio of
twelve of A. B. Frost's paintings called*
Shooting Pictures. *These handsome
lithographs, which soon became sought
after by collectors, typified the artist's
work in the outdoor genre; three of
them are shown here by courtesy of
Mr. Henry M. Reed, author of* The
A. B. Frost Book. *First is the detail
from* Autumn Grouse *on the opening
page; below is* Shooting Ducks From a
Blind; *and the overleaf is* Summer
Woodcock. *At left is a separate
painting,* Adirondack Trout Fishing.

BOOKS
WE THINK
YOU'LL LIKE

Robert Kennedy and His Times
by Arthur M. Schlesinger, Jr.
Houghton Mifflin Company
1,000 pages, 25 photographs, $19.95

In 1965 when Arthur Schlesinger wrote about John F. Kennedy in *A Thousand Days*, he called his book a memoir. This book he calls a biography, and he strives to keep a historian's distance from his subject. But Robert Kennedy was a beloved friend, and there are sections here in which Schlesinger the biographer merges with Schlesinger the participant, the advocate.

The differences between the two Kennedy brothers were more striking than their similarities. Schlesinger characterizes JFK as a Brahmin, and Robert as a puritan; John as a happy, often merry man, and Robert as a sad one who used a grim, self-mocking humor to hide pain. Both men fought hard against social injustices—John because "he found them irrational," Robert "because he found them unbearable." And Schlesinger feels that the

President was much the tougher of the two, in spite of Bobby's reputation for ruthlessness.

Many people—and not only Republicans—distrusted and disliked RFK. Lyndon Johnson was one of them, and in this case the feeling was mutual. The two men simply "could not abide each other." J. Edgar Hoover was also a Bobby hater, a singularly implacable one. The story of Hoover's persecution of Martin Luther King, carried on mostly behind the back of his boss, Attorney General Kennedy, is one of the most chilling in this book.

To read the story of Robert Kennedy and his times, as told by a distinguished historian, is to see from a new and revealing angle all the public issues we read about, argued about, guessed at, and grieved over in the fifties and sixties. The book is powerful—and sad.

**The Great American
Baseball Scrapbook**
by A. D. Suehsdorf
Random House
160 pages, approximately 250 photographs, 120 in color, $14.95

Mostly a lively nostalgic picture book of players and assorted baseball memorabilia, this scrapbook also includes a quick run-through of baseball history from 1876 to 1969, including some enchanting trivia. For instance, did you know that early baseball players had

to double as pregame ticket takers? That at one time it took nine balls to walk a batter? That for one year (1882) ballplayers were color-coded—pitchers light blue, catchers scarlet, and so forth? Only their socks showed what team they were on.

**American Caesar:
Douglas MacArthur, 1880-1964**
by William Manchester
Little, Brown & Company
816 pages, 100 photographs and an 8-page map insert, $15.00

Douglas MacArthur was a man of staggering contradictions, and in this scrupulously researched and apparently fair biography, William Manchester doesn't pretend that he can make all the conflicting pieces fit together. MacArthur's bravery was legendary, sometimes carried to the point of foolhardiness: he would never wear a helmet in combat, he refused to have a bodyguard in postwar Japan, he wouldn't even buckle his seat belt on a plane. Yet during the long, desperate fighting on Bataan, he only once made the five-minute trip from his headquarters to the battlefront to bolster the morale of his discouraged, starving troops. Bitterly, they called him "Dugout Doug."

He was, flamboyantly, a man of action, but as commander of the Army forces in the Far East he was so stunned at the news of Pearl Harbor that when

the Japanese planes appeared over Clark airfield in the Philippines nine hours later, his entire force of bombers was still just sitting there, unprotected, wing tip to wing tip. "He was a gifted leader," Manchester writes, "and his failure in this emergency is bewildering."

Nor was he any more consistent politically. After Truman removed him from command in Korea, MacArthur appealed his case in stridently reactionary speeches all over the United States, until all but his most devoted supporters began to shy away from him. And this was the same man who had virtually transformed Japan—with tact, forbearance, and his standard quotient of theatrics—from a militaristic, emperor-worshiping despotism into a liberal democracy. An astonishing man and an absorbing book.

SAMUEL ELIOT MORISON AWARD 1978
David McCullough's
THE PATH BETWEEN THE SEAS

It is very rarely that a book of history has an important impact on current events. That happy fate came to *The Path Between the Seas: The Creation of the Panama Canal*, by David McCullough (Simon & Schuster, 1977), which American Heritage is pleased to announce is the winner of this year's Samuel Eliot Morison Award. The prize is given annually for "the best book on American history by an American author that sustains the tradition that good history is literature as well as high scholarship." President Jimmy Carter has remarked repeatedly that the treaties recently concluded, whereby ownership and operation of the Canal will eventually go to Panama, would never have passed the United States Senate had it not been for McCullough's book.

This is all the more remarkable since the book is entirely historical and does not go into the current controversy over control of the Canal. "All through the Senate debates on the issue," McCullough observes, "the book was quoted again and again, and I'm pleased to say that it was quoted by both sides. Real history always cuts both ways."

McCullough first became aware of the interest *The Path Between the Seas* was exciting in Washington a year ago,

when he and his wife, Rosalee, were invited to the White House to meet the President and the First Lady. They learned that both Mr. and Mrs. Carter had read the book, and that the President was recommending it highly to the members of the Senate Committee on Foreign Relations as background for the Canal debates. In January, 1978, McCullough testified before the committee, urging approval of the treaties; meanwhile, he had been operating as a one-man lobby, at his own expense, talking to key senators about the issues involved. "I did not take sides in the book," he explains, "but afterwards I came to feel that it was my obligation to openly take a stand, and that the treaties were absolutely the right thing to do in order to insure the best use of the Canal in the future." In June, 1978, he had the pleasure of flying to Panama

with the President to observe the ceremonies there in honor of the signing of the treaties.

David McCullough grew up in Pittsburgh, where he was born in 1933. After graduation from Yale in 1955 he worked for Time Inc. until 1961, and then for three years edited a magazine published for distribution in the Arab world by the United States Information Agency. From 1964 to 1970 he was an editor with American Heritage Publishing Company, but after the success of his first book, *The Johnstown Flood* (1968), he decided to free-lance. His second book, *The Great Bridge*—about the building of Brooklyn Bridge—was an even greater success; and *The Path Between the Seas* not only was a selection of the Book-of-the-Month Club but also won the 1978 National Book Award for nonfiction as well as the Parkman Prize, given annually by the Society of American Historians for a work of history. To these honors is now added the Morison Award of $5,000 offered by American Heritage. Mr. McCullough lives in West Tisbury, Martha's Vineyard, with his wife and five children. He is now at work on a book about the youth and young manhood of Theodore Roosevelt.

In the winter of 1915, Jeff Ward, owner of "The Big Store" dry goods establishment in Tazewell, Virginia, took the train to New York City to buy up-to-date items for the coming season. His visit evidently went well and to celebrate it—and his forty-seventh birthday on February 9—he had the versatile cameraman who ran the White Way Photo Studio at 1341 Broadway make this portrait showing multiple Wards in solemn communion with themselves. He was pleased enough with the result to order postcards made up for his friends.

This photograph was sent to us by the sitter's niece, Mrs. John M. Aldrich of Roanoke. We continue to invite our readers to send us unusual, dramatic, or amusing photographs—at least thirty years old —that they own. They should be sent to Geoffrey C. Ward (no relation), American Heritage Publishing Co., 10 Rockefeller Plaza, New York, NY 10020.

As we cannot be responsible for original material, we request that a copy be sent at first. Under no circumstances should glass negatives be mailed. Pictures can be returned only if accompanied by a stamped, self-addressed envelope. AMERICAN HERITAGE will pay $50.00 for each one that is run.

SEND IN THE CLONES

ACROSS

1 ____ mer (seasickness)
6 Roof material in South America
12 Sonoran's cloak
18 Historians Will and ____ Durant
19 Carpenter's spacecraft: 1962
20 Papal capes
21 Dustin Hoffman role
22 He has pressing problems
23 Curved noses of rockets
24 "Father of the Constitution"
26 Small: Comb. form
27 Polite refusal
28 "Have You Ever ____ Lonely?"
29 "Sword of the Revolution"
31 "____ Tavern in the Town"
34 "For ____ Jolly Good Fellow"
35 Russian veto
38 ____ de combat
39 Nickname of astronaut Slayton
41 Winslow Homer medium
44 Sunday sound in Mexico City
45 Neighbor of Uru. and Bol.
46 Wounded hero decorated by 29-Across
49 Agency that electrified rural USA
50 Lake discovered by Frémont
52 Map within a map
53 One on a picket line
55 Key to heredity
57 ____ voce
59 Sonny's sibling
60 O'Neill's ____ Interlude
64 Decree in Damascus
66 Spider bugs
70 Finnish novelist: 1861–1921
71 Railroad workers' hero in 1894
74 Astronaut Evans
75 A citizen of Vientiane
76 Seaver, Rose, and other Cincy heroes
77 Hog plum of India
78 Square bolt-holder
79 Osculate
81 Wood sorrels
84 Scottish breed of dairy cattle
86 Ticonderoga hero
90 ____ Cristo-Loveanu, painter of Eisenhower
91 Of cardinals, kinglets, etc.
92 Author O'Flaherty
93 ____ Attucks, black hero killed in Boston Massacre
96 Put off indefinitely
97 Moss Hart's autobiography
99 Creator of Sherlock Holmes
100 What the busy bee spreads
101 Wobble
102 Chou ____
103 Bear witness
104 Ancient ascetic
105 Divination is their vocation

DOWN

1 Brickmaker's mixture
2 Zone
3 World hero: May, 1927
4 Units of fineness for silk
5 French president's official residence
6 Tin foil for backs of mirrors
7 Ben-____, Wallace hero
8 Redolence
9 Fashionable
10 Sight at Christmastime
11 Tippecanoe hero
12 Prominent Chinese family name
13 Bane of grain
14 ____ d'être
15 Amazing hero of W.W. I
16 Legal equal
17 Tee's predecessor
25 South Dakota city
29 Arouses
30 Indian otters
31 "____ Reminds Me," Barkley's autobiography
32 Sabra's dance
33 Truck part
36 Robert ____, CSA hero
37 "Ay, ____ her tattered ensign down!"
40 Excuse offered by a barrister's client
42 A great deal
43 Setting for Reggie Jackson's heroics: 1977
46 U.S. hero of 1976 Olympics
47 Concern of Spenser, Pope, et al.
48 ____ rima (a-b-a-b-a-b-c-c)
51 Fatima slept here
54 A distinctive theory
56 Chills and fever
58 One casting a decisive vote
60 Dr. Jonas, medical hero
61 Siamese
62 Hero of San Juan Hill
63 Heath in Hardy's Return of the Native
65 Like Poe's tales
67 Heroic newsman, killed in W.W. II
68 Tart
69 Poker player's payment
72 Increase in intensity or size
73 Less furnished
78 "____ is on me"
80 U.S. historian: 19th century
82 ____ Restaurant, 1969 film
83 Lists of nominees
85 Glissades
87 Wealthy people
88 Concerning
89 Chew the scenery
91 Cat on ____ Tin Roof
93 Membrane of a bird's beak
94 Suffix with "cell"
95 Six, in Seville
96 Where to find a pump room
98 River in England

by Eugene T. Maleska

Solution in the next issue

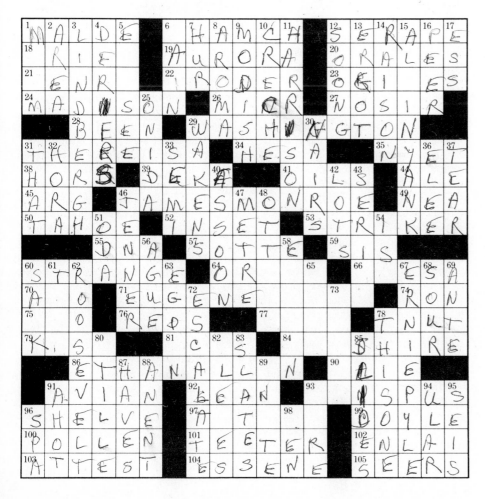

POSTSCRIPTS

"I THEN WENT HUNTING BUFFALO..."

Western pioneers, by and large, were not a wordy lot. Nor were they much given to complaint. But the following letter surely sets some sort of record for taciturnity in the face of hardship. It was written from Fort Worth, Texas, in 1878 by James Fitzwilliam, an ex-Confederate who had headed west after the Civil War, to a sister back East from whom he had just heard after a period of years. Her half of the exchange is lost, but she evidently had suffered a severe reversal of some kind and had written to see whether he might send her some money to tide her over.

His letter begins with an expression of sympathy for her "altered circumstances" and a promise to help out just as soon as he can. He, too, had had some reverses, however: he had a new job "sampling cotton," but pneumonia laid him low for a time, and he ran up some eighty dollars worth of bills with his landlady and the local doctor. And then he had some other bad luck: "My Wife and little girl was kill'd by the Indians. House and everything in it burn'd. They took 27 head of horses. I was out after cattle. When I came home everything was gone. I with 9 others took their trail and followed for 8 days. Came on the

band numbering about twenty-five. We kill'd 7 and we lost one man kill'd. I was shot in the arm with an arrow and the first-finger of my left hand was shot off. I came back to my ranch and sold out what cattle I had and what horses I had for $700 and went to New Mexico. Bought 1500 head of sheep. Drove them to Texas and the first Winter lost about 900 of them caused by Snow—cold Weather and Wolfs. Sold the remainder out for less than cost as I did not have Snow Sheds. I then went to work running cattle and worked a year. Made $300 dollars. I then went hunting Buffalo. Hunted them for three years. Quit that with about $900. Went to Henrietta Clay Co. this state and bought an interest in a Hotel. Run it about 8½ month and lost money at it. While hunting I contracted a catarrh in my nose. It has disfigured me considerable. In fact for the past five years I have had a terrible hard time."

A month later, Fitzwilliam wrote to his sister again, according to his great-grandnephew, James L. Cunningham of Des Peres, Missouri, who sent us the letter, and he enclosed the battered tintype above, displaying his maimed hand—all that he had left to remind him of his life on the frontier.

AND STRAUSS, CREATED HE THEM

Carin C. Quinn's "The Jeaning of America—and the World" in our April/May, 1978, issue brought forth some interesting sidelights. The first came from Arthur H. Hahn of Washington, D.C., who tells us that he was particularly diverted by the Levi Strauss advertisement showing Michelangelo's *David* clad in a pair of cutoff blue jeans. "It strikes me," Mr. Hahn says, "that there must be a sort of affinity of Levis for Michelangelo. Remember the great Sistine Chapel ceiling, with God's finger stretched to that of Adam? Well, some time ago, during a trip to Denmark, my wife and I saw a large billboard. Its central theme was the foregoing—except that the fingers were supporting the familiar blue denims!" The Sistine Chapel diversion was, like the *David* statue, one of a series of somewhat irreverent advertisements launched by Levi Strauss & Co. in Europe. Art lovers were not amused, however, and the series was discontinued.

A more recent advertising gimmick for the venerable pants may have better luck. It is a genuine hot-air balloon (opposite) lovingly shaped into an immense pair of blue jeans. Waist: 1160 inches; inseam: 1198 inches; patch: 108 inches by 84 inches; capacity: 65,000 cubic feet. Manufactured by Cameron Balloons Limited of Bristol, England, the balloon reportedly is floating around somewhere in the Netherlands.

Finally, we received a report from Robert White, who insists that he is the corresponding secretary for the Poor Boy Syndrome Therapy Group #1 of Billings, Montana. "Despite our general approval of Miss Quinn's story," he writes, "we regret to report that we have a Committee on Nit-Picking.... Miss Quinn states in her second paragraph that Levi Strauss invented blue jeans. Not so, our Committee contends. What Levi invented were *Levis*.... There were blue jeans around before Levi came along, and as evidence we cite ... 'Blue Jeans' Williams," who, Mr. White goes on to remind us, was governor of Indiana from 1877 until his death in office in 1880. Like many another politician of his era, Williams capitalized on his rural background and as his personal symbol chose the homespun clothing of his boyhood— Kentucky blue jeans, not only as pants but sometimes as complete suits, including one lined with silk and given to the governor by "ladies of Louisville, Kentucky."

The Poor Boy committee is quite correct about the antiquity of the term "blue jeans," of course. However, our Committee on Nit-Picking the Nit-Pickers hastens to point out that since the governor's blue jeans were made from *wool*, not the tough cotton denim that was one of the distinctive characteristics of Levi's pants, it seems to us that the ghost of Levi Strauss can rest in peace.

1928

TITLE INSURANCE & TRUST CO., LOS ANGELES

1978

DAVID STRICK/*The New York Times*

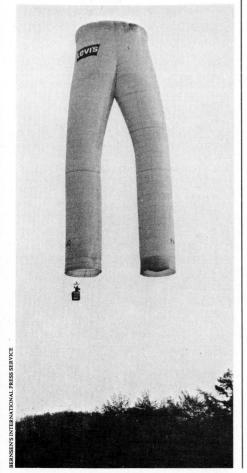

BERNSEN'S INTERNATIONAL PRESS SERVICE

For more than fifty years, the "largest sign in the world"—a city block long and four stories high— perched on the side of a hill on the edge of Griffith Park, Los Angeles, cruelly treated by time and weather. HULLY-WOD, its broken letters read most recently; not too many years ago, they read HOLLYWOOD, and before that, when it was erected to celebrate the site of a fancy subdivision in the 1920's, HOLLY-WOODLAND.

By whatever name, and however decrepit, the sign was a symbol—one of the few surviving relics of Hollywood's golden era, when the great studios were run like private fiefdoms by what author Ben Hecht called "undersized magnates," when stars were discovered sitting at drugstore counters (or sometimes on bar stools), when movie-making was still "fairy-land on a production line," as screenwriter Otis Fergusson described it.

But that Hollywood is dead, done in by television, corporate mergers and conglomerate takeovers, and the disintegration of the studio system that made the whole glamorous machine work. And the sign that symbolized it became a bit of history. To mark it as such, the Los Angeles Cultural Heri-tage Board in 1973 officially classified it Historic Cultural Monument No. 111. Unfortunately, monument status was little protection from wind and rain, which eventually reduced most of the letters of the sign to tatters. Having been declared a historic monument, it was now declared a dangerous public nuisance; it would have to come down, the authorities said. A fluttery movement to save and reconstruct the sign foundered on the $250,000 necessary to do the job. Then, this year, the cavalry, led by rock star Alice Cooper, came thundering to the rescue. He wanted to donate $27,000 to rebuild an O. Hugh Hefner promptly decided he wanted to fix the Y, Andy Williams the W, Gene Autry an L, Warner Bros. Records another O, and so on. Next month, a spanking new fixed-up sign will be unveiled. History lives in Hollywood.

THE SWEET SMELL OF HISTORY

Philip Myers, whose memories of the Gettysburg reunion of 1913 contributed greatly to Bruce Catton's "The Day the Civil War Ended" in the June/July, 1978, issue, has sent along an addendum to the story: "There was a Confederate veteran shoemaker in Westminster, Maryland, where I attended college. He had been to the reunion, so we had much in common, despite the disparity of our ages.

" 'You saw [the re-creation of] Pickett's charge,' he told me one day. 'You saw the Stars and Bars waving. You heard the Rebel Yell. But you can't claim to be a Yankee veteran if you have never smelled Confederate powder. I'll fix that.'

"In his tiny shop that winter day in 1914 a small egg stove glowed redly. He opened a chest, pulled out an envelope from which he shook some black flakes into his open hand. He drew me closer to the stove, held me tightly, and commanded: 'Smell!' A small cloud of white smoke filled the air as the gunpowder fell on the hot metal. I sniffed deeply."

THE 864-MEDAL MISUNDERSTANDING

In a "Postscripts" feature on Dr. Mary Edwards Walker and her Congressional Medal of Honor in the December, 1977, issue, we repeated the familiar story that 864 members of the 27th Maine Regiment had received medals during the Civil War "through some clerk's error," and because of that the medals were rescinded in 1917 by an Adverse Action Medal of Honor Board. Not exactly, a number of readers have pointed out. The men of the 27th Maine had been promised the medals by Secretary of War Edwin M. Stanton, with the approval of President Lincoln, in exchange for re-enlisting to bolster the defenses of Washington, D.C., during the week preceding the Battle of Gettysburg in 1863. Upon reflection, the 1917 board decided the re-enlistment did not qualify as action "above and beyond the call of duty," and forthwith stripped the down-Easters of the nation's highest military honor.

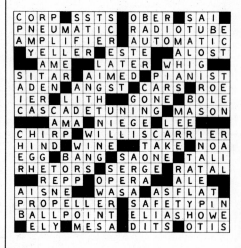

Solution to the August/September Crossword Puzzle

Congressional Medal of Honor, Civil War vintage
NATIONAL ARCHIVES